# Poetry

## from the

# Edge

### Mitch Salmon

TRUTH BOOK PUBLISHERS

ISBN   978-1-935298-51-9

Truth Book Publishers
824 Bills Rd
Franklin, IL  62638
877-649-9092
truthbookpublishers@yahoo.com
www.truthbookpublishers.com

First Printing 2010

Printed in the United States of America

1. Book - Religion   2. Poetry   3. Devotional

This book is dedicated to Jesus

He is my master, my redeemer and my best friend

# Foreword

On April 21st of 2009 my entire life changed in a very real way. It was on this day that God bridged the widest gap I had ever known… the distance from my head to my heart. For years I had been trying to live up to a religious standard. I knew who God was. I had heard about His love thousands of times. I had even committed my life to Jesus. Still, I didn't truly know Him.

I heard Him call me to the floor of my Denver hotel room. I might have normally resisted or even ignored Him. However, on this day I was far too broken to fight. I had given up on every-thing, including me. All of my self righteous efforts to meet His standards had failed. I was nothing but a pile of worn out, dirty rags. As I fell time and time again I would pick myself up, stiffen my resolve to live according to His will, and set myself back on course. That was the way that I saw it. In reality my entire life was swirling through the cycle of shame. I was attempting to find the One True God by going through the motions. I was attempting to do what I thought was right through my own power. I was trying to change from the outside in what could only be changed from the inside out.

God met me on the floor of that hotel room. He spoke the words of healing that I had longed to hear for years. I had to be truly broken to be made whole. I had to eliminate my self efforts as a way of achieving His love. I was bought with a high price and now I am not my own. I am His.

It was the very next morning that I began writing. I have been writing ever since. I had lived life behind a mask for so many years. I had been hiding the real me. Like most people, I was afraid of being rejected. I was afraid of being found out for who I truly was. Like so many other Christians, I had been playing make believe. His love and total acceptance allowed me to become real with Him, with myself, and with the rest of the world. With His instruction I started a group on Facebook called "Behind The Curtain." The hiding was over. Darkness runs from the light and His light began shining brightly through me!

For the last eighteen months I have been a witness to God's true power. I have seen lives change. I have seen that gap that was within me (the one between the head and the heart) bridged many times in the lives of others. I was transformed from an introspective, self absorbed perfectionist to an ambassador of His love.

If you are reading this book today, I want you to know that it is NO ACCIDENT. God has a deeper love for you than you could possibly imagine. I could write a thousand pages about it and still not make it clear to you. I encourage you to find out for yourself. I don't know your past but it doesn't matter. He wants you to know that you are NOT the sum total of your actions. You are not meant to be identified by your shame. He knows your true identity and He longs to reveal it to you. He waits for you. He waits for the answer that He longs most to hear. The answer is "yes!"

So, friend, as you read my heartfelt words I encourage you to consider for yourself who He is. Look deep inside as you to seek these answers within your own heart. It is when we seek with our heart that we will find. Your Heavenly Father is standing on the porch of His home. He is looking far down the path leading to Him. He is waiting for you to come to Him. His arms are not crossed in anger. They are open and ready to embrace you. He is waiting to throw a robe of around your shoulders. He is waiting to adorn your finger with His ring of love. He has a fattened calf ready for your homecoming. You are His beloved child and He can't wait to celebrate your homecoming. Love, mitch

# Poetry

## from the

## Edge

### Mitch Salmon

## A Journey to Grace

Traveling down life's long road,
I reach a fork in the path I pursue.
I scan ahead in both directions,
uncertain of what I should do.

One path is worn from many a traveler.
The other appears to be overgrown.
Two paths to select from,
yet only one will lead me home.

I choose the path to the right,
and am able to walk with ease.
Soon enough I reach my destination,
A door that reads, "The God you will please."

Turning the knob I step into the room inside.
It took a few minutes to adjust to the light.
Now I see a masked man standing before me.
I ask how he is and he says, "I'm alright."

Looking around this vast room,
all masks with various dispositions.
Each of them seems to be "alright."
I wish not to be an imposition.

In this room a banner is raised high
It reads, "Striving to please God."
I am in agreement with creed,
and involuntarily give a subtle nod.

Mingling throughout this room,
I interact with each person behind their mask.
My tendency to be introverted slowed me,
so introducing myself proved quite a task

Most of the masks were adorned with smiles.
Each and every person said they were alright.
There had to be something more to this story.
I knew that it would eventually come to light.

As I stood along the wall observing,
through one man's mask I could see a crack.
A few salty tears slid down the front of it.
He seemed powerless to hold them back.

Suddenly a shrill piercing scream rang out,
as he shouted for all to hear, "I'm not alright!"
"I can't live by this creed and neither can any of you!"
"I want out of this room and am ready to fight!"

Suddenly he bolted for the door.
Still in shock, I turned and quickly followed.
Slamming the door behind us on our exit;
this place sounded good and yet it felt so hollow!

Safely outside he cast aside his mask,
so that I could finally see his true face.
The expressions I saw told a story by themselves.
He motioned and we turned from this place.

As we journeyed back down this road,
the one that was paved with good intentions,
we spoke in honesty with one another
casting aside our fears, releasing our tensions.

He told me how for years he had strived
to fulfill the motto that hung on that wall.
But each time that he thought he had mastered it
he would suddenly trip again and fall.

Meanwhile we passed the fork and turned;
only one choice of path remained.
At first it was rocky and steep
and the traveling was a bit strained.

As we continued the road became smooth.
It ended at an old wooden shack.
We were uncertain as to what we should do
but knew it was too late to turn back.

Apprehension flooded through us
as we began to open the door.
From the looks on the faces within
we knew we hadn't been here before.

Every feeling was out in the open.
There was a deep peace that filled this place.
The banner that hung on this wall said
"Welcome to the room of grace!"

No more the air of pretentiousness.
No more pretending to be "alright."
Love and joy flooded throughout.
We were overcome at the very sight!

Sweet music of praise filled the air.
It was apparent these people were free.
They did not hide their flaws from others.
Instead they let them out for all to see.

Love and acceptance replaced the façade.
We were warmly welcomed in.
I suddenly felt inadequacy creep up inside
but heard, "Grace can even cover that sin!"

So here is where we decided to stay
and we hope never to leave.
Except to go back to that old room
and find a few people we can retrieve!

I first discovered this "room of grace" through a book I read, aptly entitled, "TrueFaced." I remember my first pass through the book. As I read I was filled with doubt. I found myself thinking things like, "This couldn't possibly be. What about pleasing God?" To be honest with you, I cast it aside as a fairytale. Sure all of this sounded great, but there was no way that I could believe that God would be satisfied with just "me" as an offering. He wanted my blood, sweat and tears! He wanted my endless striving, self loathing, and shame! However, when God spoke my name last year and changed me from the inside out, He also affirmed for me that this "room of grace" was truth! I didn't doubt it anymore. No longer was I going to strive to reach this point of sin management where I would be acceptable to God. I already was! I took my eyes off of my sin and instead focused them directly on Him. His love and grace changed my life. They can change yours as well! Are you tired of striving to reach that place where you think you will be acceptable? Have you determined that you will never measure up to His standard? I invite you this morning to THINK AGAIN!

Chris Tomlin did an adaptation of the original song, "Amazing Grace." He added a chorus that says, "My chains are gone. I've been set free. My God, my Savior has ransomed me. And like a flood, His mercy reigns. Unending love, amazing grace." So, are you wrapped in chains? Are they weighing you down? Do you wish to break free? Are you ready to accept this gift? It's not called AMAZING grace for nothing! It is amazing indeed!

## Adoration Of The King

Early in the morning I rise
with your praises on my tongue.
I am reminded of your goodness and grace
with each breath I draw into my lungs.

You are my Master;
my gentle yet most powerful King.
If I did not cry out your praises
then surely the rocks would sing!

As I look out into the east
I anticipate the rising of the morning sun.
The new light on the horizon
reminds me of the battle over darkness won.

Each new day is filled with promise;
Your undying love for me apparent now.
Salty tears of joy stream down my cheeks
as again before You I bow.

Over my shoulder I see the scorched earth;
it's withered and dry statues were once life.
I traveled through this land alone.
I experienced nothing but loneliness and strife.

Before me the green grass waves with the breeze
In the midst of it, a gently flowing spring.
I drink from the cool, clear waters
I soak in the refreshment that it brings.

I could remain in this place forever
Your felt presence fills my heart with peace.
The utterances on my tongue are Yours
I pray that they will never cease.

I wonder if You would show Yourself
so that I may gaze directly into Your eyes.
I fall at Your feet my beloved Father
Your truth dispelled the enemy's darkest lies!

No more parched throat thirsting
No more withering away in the heat.
You dealt a mighty blow to the enemy
and he was put down in defeat!

With my knees I bow before you.
With my tongue I willingly confess.
When you call me out by my name
may my answer always be "Yes!"

For the past 6 months my soul has been in the desert. Everything felt dry, lifeless, and empty. I struggled to get out of bed in the morning. I wondered if there was any point to writing to our group and whether anyone really even read my words. I cried out time and time again to be freed of this place, not knowing why I had come to it. It seemed cruel to the point of being unbearable. These were my FEELINGS. As I continued to discern the truth from lies, I realized that I had been to this place before. Each time I found myself feeling empty I began pointing fingers at myself. I began questioning my value. Eventually I would throw in the towel on God after deciding I would never hear His voice again. This trip through the desert was different. Although all of the feelings I shared there, I decided to cling to the truth of His love. I decided that although I hated this place, I trusted God enough to stop pointing fingers.

This morning I sit on the far side of this desert. The grass is greener than I can ever recall. The water is fresh and clean. The birds are singing their merriment and the clouds drift lazily overhead through a sky hued in the most incredible color of blue. I realize that this experience in the desert has been like no other I have ever faced. I bent, sure, but I did not break! This may sound strange, but my eyes tear up every time I think of the desert that lies behind me. I realize as I look back upon it that I am thankful for having been there! The truth does NOT change. It remains constant, EVEN in the face of our feelings. So this morning, where are you? Are you enjoying the lush green grass? If so, thank God for it! Are you standing in the midst of a vast wasteland not sure if you will make it to the other side? If that is the case, lean into His love! I know the desert and so I am glad to be your guide. God is trustwor-thy ALL of the time! Need someone to talk to? Are you afraid to share the truth about where you are in your life? I'm here and I promise to lend you an ear free of judgment and FILLED with love. I share these truths from the depths of my heart. Love, mitch.

## *An Audience With the King*

All alone in this place,
yet there is no peace to be found.
Loneliness is yet another chain
with which I have been bound.

Time stands still before me
even as the earth continues to move.
Sometimes I find myself running hard
as though I have something to prove.

If I were only a little better
then I would finally be worthy of attention.
I squabble as though there were not enough
I doubt I have a name worthy of mention.

Will you look down upon me now?
Will you enter into this lonely place?
Whether I stare at moon or at sun
I wish only to see your face.

I know that you indwell the heavens
But would you also be with me here?
My heart has only one true desire;
that you would draw near.

So I decide to seek you on the mountain top
I continue my search down into the valley.
I search for you out on the busy streets
I look for you down every dark alley.

Would you hide yourself from me?
Would you turn the other way?
It feels as though the sun is blotted out.
There is no light amidst this day.

Where is your heart, my Lord?
How do I find my way there?
My glass is more than half empty
I search my cupboards but they're bare.

How can these words feed a nation
when they don't begin at the heart of you?
I look to articulate with meaning
yet you represent all that is true.

May those who struggle for meaning
find it in your mercy and grace.
May you show yourself plainly before us
so that we may see your face.

Over the past year of fielding private responses to posts on the group, the most commonly asked questions I read are, "Where is God? Does he know about my plight? Does he care?" We want evidence of his presence. We want just some small sign to show that he loves us enough to enter into our places of deepest pain. There is one who lived through all of these things and remained true to his father. His name is Jesus and he DOES understand our plight. Do you feel his presence in your life today?

Do you feel like you are less than enough? Do you have skeletons hanging in your closet that you wish you could share? Do you feel a deep need for healing in your life? Do you wish to trade shame for peace? You are NOT alone!

## Answered Prayer

With head held high
I praise the Lord's name aloud.
I hold my hands to the sky
My actions are openly proud.
I am dressed for show
in all of my finest attire.
I know you will curse my foe
but I am too righteous for the fire.
I thank God for my righteousness
and that I am an upstanding man.
I would never bother to confess
the evil committed by my hand.
I give my ten percent tithe
and worship here each week.
Never worrying if my soul is alive
nor the Lord's grace do I seek.
I glance to my right
and see a man poorly dressed.
I am glad not to share his plight
nor to have HIS sins to confess.
Tears stream down his cheeks
and it is clear that he is a sinner.
The perfume of his flesh reeks
not the type I would invite to dinner.
His head is held low
with his face on the floor.
It appears his life has been dealt a blow
and he is shaken to the core.
What sin did this man commit
that causes his obvious weeping?
Surely he is receiving what he should get.
What commandment wasn't he keeping?
He walks with head down to the door
never uttering a single sound.

Only his tears remain on the floor
where he knelt on hallowed ground.
Only one of these men was blessed
with an answer to their prayers.
Was it the man who confessed?
Or the one with hands in the air?
The Lord loves the humble.
He gives mercy to the meek.
He knows that we will stumble;
forgives when its His will we seek.


He told his next story to some who were complacently pleased with themselves over their moral performance and looked down their noses at the common people: *"Two men went up to the Temple to pray, one a Pharisee, the other a tax man. The Pharisee posed and prayed like this: 'Oh, God, I thank you that I am not like other people—robbers, crooks, adulterers, or, heaven forbid, like this tax man. I fast twice a week and tithe on all my income.'*

*"Meanwhile the tax man, slumped in the shadows, his face in his hands, not daring to look up, said, 'God, give mercy. Forgive me, a sinner.'"*

Jesus commented, *"This tax man, not the other, went home made right with God. If you walk around with your nose in the air, you're going to end up flat on your face, but if you're content to be simply yourself, you will become more than yourself."* (Luke 18: 9-14)

False pride is one the most "acceptable" of sins in the church. Yet this behavior among Christians is the first thing to push outsiders away. We who have known the Lord for years sometimes have a tendency of losing our perspective. Instead of relying on grace we begin looking at our own righteousness. How is it that we forget the pit we came out of? One thing is for sure, those who walk with their head held high are likely to miss the holes that lie before them. If you are in need of grace, know that the Lord waits for your cries! He will show mercy to you and make you whole. So, think about this honestly. Who are you in this story? Are you the self-righteous man or the sinner in touch with your failures? God promises to humble the proud and raise the humble.

## *Basking In Glory*

In the trees and in the flowers
In the voice that's carried on the wind.
Your words are rest for the weary.
They are truth that knows no end.

From yesterday's death and decay
comes today's rejuvenating growth.
The colors of the rainbow over head,
A renewing of Your oath.

The clouds bring their healing rains.
They fall upon all those who thirst.
The righteous and the wicked alike
will see evidence of the storm burst.

Standing out fully in the light
witnessing the radiance of the sun.
Day always conquers the night
to remind us that the battle is won.

Walk with me here in the garden.
may my presence be a delight.
Standing in the open unashamed
visible to You in plain sight.

So I invite you to gaze upon me.
I know what you will see.
Once a prisoner wrapped in chains;
now fully alive and free.

We were made to live in freedom, not captivity. Even the death and decay of the past can be used. These hurts help us to see how much we need redemption and how much we desire freedom. Jesus came so that we may be free, not barely free, abundantly free!

Do you know his healing power?

## Beacon On the Hill

Traveling down this road
the going was getting tough.
All of my striving to make progress
never quite seemed to be enough.
So often I had stumbled
upon many a loose stone.
Some said they were beside me
but inside I still felt so alone.

My knees were scratched and bruised
from so many a fall.
I often cried out for assistance
but heard no answer to my call.

When another path presented itself
doubt and confusion entered my mind.
Scratching my head in uncertainty;
I decided to leave the rugged road behind.

This choice seemed much smoother;
nary a stone to obstruct my stride.
Yet this path was not on my map.
Panic over being lost welled up inside.

Still I continued forward
one hurried step at a time.
I was so busy looking ahead
that I never considered what was behind.

When finally I looked over my shoulder
the path traveled had been overgrown.
No choice remained but to continue onward;
and there was no doubt that I was alone.

The sun faded into shadows
and shadows eventually gave way to night.
Now my steps were taken in blindness.
The path was completely devoid of light.

I stopped and stood;
then finally sat down in my despair.
All around nothing but ink blackness
and I was no longer traveling anywhere.

As my circumstances overwhelmed me;
looking to the hills, the appearance of a star.
As the only light it became my focus;
yet it seemed to be off so far.

I said a silent prayer in my fear.
I prayed for His forgiveness of my transgression.
I found myself vowing to be true
and promising that I learned my lesson.

So I set out in a new direction;
the shortest between myself and the hill.
All the while still whispering prayers
praying that this would be His will.

Now only brush surrounded me.
Each step taken was deliberate and slow.
Still many times I stumbled;
and picked myself up from the thorns below.

I paused for a brief respite
and to take a few deep breaths.
It was then that I could hear something.
I was sure it was another's footsteps.

I cried out in a greeting
before doubt could muffle my sound.
I heard a response echo back.
I was not the only one traveling this ground!

Although there was no seeing in this darkness
I took solace in the fact that I was not alone in my plight.
It was then that I heard many more footsteps;
a multitude struggling towards the light.

I looked back to the hill above
and noticed I had not been seeing a star.
It was someone holding a beacon up
so that it could be seen from afar.

Many weary travelers
came along close to my side.
We each spoke of our ill-fated journeys.
Unto each other we began to confide.

Many broken paths we had traveled;
each of them leading to one hill.
Once we were shattered and lost
we became willing to bend to His will.

All these paths were converging
until they became only one.
There is only one way to the Father
and it passes directly through the Son.

Yes, they led back to the rocky road.
The same one we left sometime before.
Yet we were shown the way back home
and in the end we were restored.

When I was given the vision of this group I had no aspirations of perfection for myself or anyone else. As a matter of fact, it was the contrary. I was being led to expose my flaws and let others know, "It's OK. We all have them." In finding that we are not alone, we can discover strength. In hearing about someone else's pain we can both relate and learn from their experiences. We find ourselves on this rocky road. Some are returning to it. Some are finding it for the first time. Either way, we want it to be smooth. We want it to be easy. The truth is, it isn't. Although this road leads to the perfect destination, it is an imperfect and windy path. Progress can be slow. The rocks we stumble on bring pain to our lives. Maybe we brought it on ourselves. Maybe it comes as a result of circumstances beyond our control. Either way, we have a choice of isolating ourselves or leaning on others. In leaning on others we often find they are on the same path, headed in the same direction. We find that they too have experienced points of extreme pain. Maybe the circumstances of our pain differ, but the feelings are pretty much the same. So are you traveling this road alone? Maybe you are new to it. Maybe you are still trying to find your way out of the woods. There is a beacon on the highest hill. He is the way, the truth and the life. His name is Jesus. Wherever you are, look up and you can find him there!

## Behind The Curtain

The stage is set.
The curtain is drawn.
The audience is watching.
The show must go on.

Actors to their places;
each striking their assigned pose.
They project their various characters
through carefully rehearsed prose.

The audience is thrilled.
They thoroughly enjoyed the show.
As the curtain closes
They turn and begin to go.

Now only the actors remain
without the benefit of memorized parts.
The rush of the performance settles
as they ponder in their hearts.

Did the show seem real?
Had the audience truly believed?
With the burden of false pretense behind
surely they would be relieved.

Yet there was an awkward silence.
Hardly a word was spoken.
A soft sobbing noise burst forth
and the silence was suddenly broken.

The actor played the funny man
but he wasn't laughing anymore.
His face was visibly streaked
as the tears began to pour.

On the stage he brought humor,
yet behind the curtain he was hurting.
He tried to silence his sobs
but couldn't control the blurting.

How would these performers act
amidst this unrehearsed reality?
Most continued to cling to their masks
not knowing what it means to be free.

Yet one stagehand took notice.
His heart felt for the funny man's pain.
He was nothing in the big show
and had no reasons to be vain.

Not knowing the nature of hurt,
indeed he had no clue,
he wrapped his arms around the actor,
saying, "Jesus loves you too."

Several seconds passed
before this false funny man spoke.
He could barely compose himself.
On his words he began to choke.

"How could he love a man like me?"
"Of what possible value am I to God?"
"I feel as though I will explode inside."
"How could he forgive me for this façade?"

Even through his doubt
it seemed he was able to believe.
As the look on his face changed
and he suddenly seemed relieved.

Now the funny man began laughing a real laugh
as it was clear joy had filled him from the inside.
No longer would he bear the weight of this mask
No longer would he seek to hide.


You pay the fee for the ticket. You take your seat. You watch the show. When the actor is on the stage they are paid to play a part. Their character knows the right things to say and every action they will take. It's all carefully choreographed and repeatedly rehearsed but it is not real.

Behind the Curtain is an invitation to get beyond the characters we play and find the REAL. We are all searching for answers but we won't find them in the show. We will find them behind the curtain. Come on in and seek openly and honestly. Do you crave true love that can never be stolen from you? Do seek mercy and forgiveness for past mistakes? Do you seek to trade your shame for an abiding peace? Pull back the curtain and enter!

We are here to place transparency before hypocrisy. We are here to love rather than judge. God sees us all for who we are anyway! Sooner or later the show ends. Sooner or later the curtain is drawn. Sooner or later we find ourselves with no more memorized lines to repeat. What remains is reality. What remains cannot be hidden or acted through. "We throw open our doors to God and discover at the same moment that he has already thrown open his door to us. We find ourselves standing where we always hoped we might stand—out in the wide open spaces of God's grace and glory, standing tall and shouting our praise." Romans 5:2

Bring others to find out what's BEHIND THE CURTAIN!

## Bursting At The Seams

The seams are stretching;
about to tear.
The weight of this burden;
more than I can bare.

Cannot shake the feeling;
cannot break free.
Running is a futile pursuit
when there is nowhere to flee.

The skeletons are in the closet
I cringe in front of the door.
Head heavy in my hands;
tears covering the floor.

The seams now bursting;
tearing apart a thread at a time.
Is there grace for a sinner like me?
Death the penalty for my crimes.

I cower now in the shadows;
naked and ashamed.
I point my finger to myself;
for I am the one to blame.

Fighting the demons in my mind;
all my might not enough.
I fall to my knees again
when the going gets tough.

Dare not to hope
when all hope has been lost.
Yet if it could be purchased
I would pay any cost.

Hear my urgent cries!
Do not forsake me now!
I don't deserve to hear your voice
but I must find it somehow.

A long moment of silence;
amidst my greatest pain.
I cry out for His forgiveness
and grace falls like rain.

No punishment for the fall.
The shame will not prevail.
The winds of His perfect love
come to fill my sail.

What keeps you from allowing others behind your own personal curtain?

## Call of the Savior

Come to me all of you who are weary
Come to me all of you who are broken.
Come sit at my feet
And hear these words that are spoken.

For my yoke is easy
And my burden is light.
Although I may seem distant
I will lead you in this fight.

Sin dealt man a fateful blow.
and from grace you have fallen.
Yet it was for you that I bore suffering
so that you could hear my calling.

There is no place that you can run.
There is no place that you can hide.
You may not know me now
but in me you can confide.

I will be faithful until the end.
I will catch you when you fall.
I am here and will answer your cries
when you humble yourself and call.

Oh father
who lives in heaven above.
Oh how I long for your healing.
How I crave your eternal love!

Come into my heart today
and free me from this pain.
May your kingdom come to earth.
May you forever reign.

Oh Lord!
I will make you the king of my heart.
I will turn myself over to you today.
I want to make a fresh start!

Now that you are mine
I will be evident in you.
I embrace you with arms wide
Now make many of the few.

The path may be narrow
but I will walk it ahead.
And when you hunger for me
rest assured that you will be fed.

For I am the God of the poor
I am the protector of the persecuted.
My words are in the wind and waves
and they cannot be muted.

Now go out into this world
and show others the love I freely give
I shed my blood on that day
So that you might live.


It's easy to discount these words and believe that is God is distant. It's easy to come to the conclusion that he doesn't care about the trials we face. Maybe you have already decided that you are going to live this life on your own. I talk daily to very lonely and broken people who are right here among us. Some have been wronged and have seen no justice. Others are broken on the inside. There are a number of reasons we are a shattered people yet there is only one King. He can sweep up the pieces of your life and make you whole. Will you trust him today? Why continue to trudge from day to day alone? I urge you to live! I urge you to surrender yourself to the one who will complete you! I invite you to e-mail me. I invite you to bear your heart. You hear mine often enough to know that there will be no judgment. I know what it is to be broken, but I also know what it is to be whole. As I say often, we all have a choice. Make yours today!

## Come to Me

The riches of this earth
attract our eyes and create lust,
We desire the things we cannot have,
and ignore what is right and just.

What is the price of a soul?
What is the cost of this lie?
Do we not understand
that we will surely die?

To gain the world,
we are willing to lose our soul.
Yet we are completely unable
to fill the God shaped hole.

Nothing on this earth can satisfy
nothing in the world will save.
Our wicked and wanton hearts
from death and the grave.

Believing the lies,
we continue to trudge forward.
Sure that the next hill will bring peace
our earthly treasures we hoard.

Do you not know
that heavens and earth will pass away?
We will all stand and make an account
on judgment day.

So will you continue
to chase this restless wind?
Will you believe in lies
until the bitter end?

Will you both live
and die by the sword?
Or will you turn your heart
to honor our Lord?

Oh child!
He cries your name today.
He beckons you to come close
and not to go away.

Heed his call,
answer that still small voice.
We are made free
and each will make a choice.

Hail the King
who's word endures forever.
Who's love is given freely
so that our bond will not sever.

Do you know him?

Matthew 24:35 *"Heaven and earth will pass away, but my words will never pass away."*

Matthew 6: 19-21 *"Do not store up for yourselves treasures on earth, where moth and rust destroy, and where thieves break in and steal. But store up for yourselves treasures in heaven, where moth and rust do not destroy, and where thieves do not break in and steal. For where your treasure is, there your heart will be also."*

Matthew 16:26 *"What good will it be for a man if he gains the whole world, yet forfeits his soul? Or what can a man give in exchange for his soul?"*

Matthew 26:52 *"Put your sword back in its place," Jesus said to him, "for all who draw the sword will die by the sword."*

I am guilty! We are all guilty! We may not be worthy of grace, but we can still receive it! If you heart is troubled, there is salvation!

## Conversion

Walking down this road of life;
all dirt and gravel.
A bright light appears before me
and my world is unraveled.

With my eyes I see nothing
but in my heart I see your face
I was errant in my direction
yet you extend to me your grace.

I cannot continue to travel
without the benefit of sight.
The brightest light ever known
is followed by the darkest night.

I fall to my knees
and I cry out your name.
I know that you called me first
and life will never be the same.

Blind as I am
I feel you reach out your hand.
You assure that you will guide me
out of this barren land.

The journey will not be easy.
The path will not always be clear.
Yet with my trust fully in you
I will set aside my doubt and fear.

You show me the price you paid
to erase all of my sin.
No longer will I live for myself.
You will make me a fisher of men.

In my ignorance I was your enemy.
Now enlightened, you call me friend.
The scales on my eyes fall away.
No longer will I drift with the wind.

With eyes wide open seeing clearly
you guide me to the blind.
To demonstrate your love and mercy;
to show the God who is kind.


     The Apostle Paul didn't start out with that name. He was originally known as Saul of Tarsus. He was a Pharisee who worked for the Jewish clergy as a well respected leader. For all intents and purposes he was considered an educated, pious and religious man. However, Saul was misguided. His mission was false. He was traveling on the road to Damascus to arrest a group of Christians when his ignorance was revealed. A voice from heaven called out to him, "Saul, Saul, why are you out to get me?" I'm sure that Saul was confused. He worked for the church. He thought that his mission was just. Yet he was working against God. In the flash of light from heaven he was blind physically, but for the first time the truth had been revealed to him. He clearly saw the path that he had been traveling. His life was never the same after that day. Even his name changed. No longer was he known as Saul of Tarsus, persecutor of Christians. He was converted to Paul, a true Christ follower! (See Acts Chapter 9)

     Do you find yourself traveling on the road of good intentions? Who or what is guiding you? Do you proceed with clear vision or have you lost your way? There are many roads, but only one path to a more abundant life. If you find yourself heading the wrong way it's not to late to make a U-turn!

## Covered in Love

The sky above is dark and gray
but the ground is blanketed in white.
It covers our sin and iniquity;
removes our transgressions from sight.

You are faithful to cover us
with your perfect love.
Remove what is left of me
and blanket me from above.

The battle is still being fought
but the victory is already won.
Soon the storm clouds will part
revealing the light of the sun.

Your brilliance will not be hidden
when we see it with our own eyes
Your foundation is of truth and love
bringing us out of the shadow of lies.

You will not hide from us
when we earnestly seek your face.
Now come down amongst your people
and meet us in this place.

We stand in gratitude
with our arms reaching high.
We seek your perfect will
as we continue looking to the sky.


In a new year I find new hope. I look back upon the previous
year and think of all of the mistakes that I made and how I desire
not repeat them this year. At the same time I can see how God's

perfect love and grace has covered up my transgressions. It is like the fresh white snow that covers the ground. What lies beneath can no longer be seen. It is replaced with the purity of HIS perfect love!

If you do not know this kind of forgiveness, I want to let you know that it is free for the asking. God doesn't stand there with His arms crossed waiting to judge you. He stands there with His arms wide open waiting for you to call His name! Will you let HIS perfect love and grace cover you?

## Crying Inside

He paints on his best smile again.
Carefully engineered to hide,
all the secret pain that lies within.
And He's crying inside.

Her pregnancy ended before it should have.
She's convincing herself it was justified.
Yet the barren womb inside reminds her.
And she is crying inside.

His hope fails along with his marriage.
He has no one with whom to confide.
The emptiness of his life consumes him.
And he is crying inside.

He hit her yet again.
Even after promises that a cool head would preside.
Her swollen eye reminds her of his hurt.
And she is crying inside.

He stands on a lonely street corner
with no home in which to reside.
His hunger pangs him constantly.
And he is crying inside.

Her past is catching her again.
She just can't seem to swallow her pride.
Yet the memories of yesterday haunt her.
And she is crying inside.

He feels another prick from the needle.
He sometimes wishes he had died.
The euphoria of his drug can't dull the pain.
And he is crying inside.

Her shame drove her to the church today.
The judgment she felt made her leave in a hurried stride.
She convinced she will never find healing for her soul.
And she is crying inside.

His loneliness brought him to his knees today
to seek truth among all of the world's lies.
He found healing in his earnest prayers.
And he is no longer crying inside.

Her feelings of insignificance haunt her
But hopes that there is a place where her heart can abide.
She falls to her knees and lays her burdens down.
And she is no longer crying inside.


      When this message was laid on my heart it was one that I easily identified with. I fit in well among this cast of characters. I have been broken and felt that I was beyond repair. I have felt a deep hopelessness that has driven me to the edge of what I thought I could handle. The way I see it, it tends to work something like this. We experience pain. Often this pain is due to someone else's actions. We naturally seek relief from all of this hurt, but for people like me, we do it in the wrong places. The results of our poor choices are even more pain which is now heaped on top of what we initially sought to avoid. In the pursuit of freedom we shackle ourselves with even more chains. The bondage of our sin is no freedom at all! For those of you reading and identifying with these feelings, I want you to know that there is hope. There is NOTHING you can do that will separate you from Christ's love. The question is, will you hold onto the lies or will you believe the truth?

## Desert Rain

A single, small seed
buried beneath the earth.
Surrounded by dirt and dust
not realizing it's worth.

Yet it lies dormant for months.
and remains completely unchanged.
Oh how it wishes for the water
to cover this dry, desert range.

Not sure what will burst forth
and yet no longer willing to contain.
A mighty tree grows inside
yet it is not revealed without the rain.

All is parched in this drought
so that nothing is able to grow.
Only hot sun and arid winds prevail.
They continue to bake and to blow.

This small seed prays not to be discovered
beneath the shifting of these sands.
Wild creatures scour for sustenance
roaming throughout all of this land.

To be dug up now
would end its meaning and purpose.
So it continues hiding silently
somewhere beneath the surface.

Then one day it can feel the moisture
as it gathers like a sweet kiss in the air.
The waiting may be nearly over
but it seems like more than it can bear.

Clouds gather throughout the valley.
They can be seen from miles away.
For years they had been on course
to come together on this day.

First one drop falls
Then it is followed by another few.
Blowing dust is finally laid to rest
The water begins falling as if on cue.

What had been lacking for so long
begins bursting forth in great abundance.
Rain pouring down upon the desert
As if the clouds were pierced with a lance.

Without latency or hesitation
the seed bursts forth from the ground.
Green stems shoot forth in abundance.
By this earth they are no longer bound.

All across this vast desert
flowers are coming into bloom.
Honey bees seek their sweet richness.
and carry it home for their young to consume.

The carpet of color across this arid desert
transforms the very land.
No longer just an arid dust bowl
covered with nothing but shifting sand.


        This past weekend I had big plans. I felt like I was
disconnected from God and I decided that I was going to head up
into the mountains with the hopes of alleviating distractions and
focusing on Him. Things didn't quite work out as planned... but
that's a differ-ent story. I was playing worship music on Saturday
and was sur-prised at the reaction I had when this song came on.
It embodied my prayers. As I felt dry and parched (only a feeling
mind you) what I was really praying for... RAIN.

## Desires Of The Heart

I can still feel the warmth of your hand.
It brought such a deep peace.
You used it to open my prison cell.
You used it to orchestrate my release.

Yet today it seems so distant;
almost like awaking from a dream.
All does not feel well with my soul.
Nothing is quite as it seems.

I retrace my steps along this road
Hoping to find where two sets became one.
The light is fading fast around me
I long only for the brilliance of the Son.

To hear the words from your lips;
my only remaining desire.
To feel the presence of your Spirit;
the way that it sets me on fire.

This tiny candle flame wavered
in the strong gusts of wind.
Will you give me the words
or is this the end?

If I could only find that place
where the two sets of foot prints part.
If I could reach that point again
I would have a new place to start.

Are you high atop the holy mountain?
Have you removed your presence from me?
I pray you remove the scales from these eyes
so that once again I may truly see.

Life giving water is leaking from
this broken vessel, this cracked pot.
Yet I will not posture or pretend.
I am unwilling to be anything I am not.

So the world should know
of all of the highs and the lows.
The waves crash against this hull.
It cannot withstand the constant blows.

Shall I capsize and sink
amidst this vast sea of sorrow?
Or shall I hold onto truth
while anxiously awaiting the morrow?

Oh my God, my Savior!
Plant my feet firmly on the ground.
Point the path on which I travel
to the place where you can be found.


When I wrote this poem on Friday, I was in anguish. I had
been sick for over a week and was already run down. My physical
struggles led to emotional and spiritual struggles as I felt isolated
and alone. I have become used to being the sympathetic ear that
listens and offers encouragement in other's times of trouble. What
I haven't been accustomed to is reaching out in times where I am
struggling. After I wrote this, I did just that. I shared this poem
with a handful of people. I added to it, as best I could, the empti-
ness and doubt that I was experiencing. As I hovered over the send
key I had second thoughts. I wondered what people would think.
I wondered if they would judge me for my apparent lack of faith
in my struggles. I wondered how or if they would even respond. I
fought my fear… I hit send. What followed was a weekend of kind
e-mails of encouragement and hope as my friends, my brothers
and sisters, lifted me up. There was no judgment. There was no
condemnation. There was only love.

How are you this morning? Maybe you can identify with the words of my poem. Maybe, like me, you are wondering if you can reach out to anyone. Friend, let me tell you this. We were made for community! Hiding in dark corners with masks covering our pain won't solve anything. Prayer and confession will. I wonder what my state of mind would be this morning if I hadn't turned this over to the Master and confessed it to a handful of people. Chances are the same struggles would have remained and I would be in a similar state as I was on Friday. What are you holding onto this morning? You have this opportunity everyday, but today I want to give you an invitation to share. If you don't want to do it on the discussion board, that's fine. E-mail me or e-mail a few friends that you can trust. Whatever you do, don't go it alone!

## Dispelling the Lies

Looking over the mirror of my shoulder;
seeing the destruction of all these years.
Futility in chasing selfish goals;
avoiding all which causes fear.

Yet within this chase
life lost all its luster.
Continued chasing shadows
with all I could muster.

With each illusion that passed
a new one would appear.
Never quite attainable
yet always so near.

The lies in my head
continued to hem me in.
I lusted for this false joy
in a battle I could not win.

The giant stood before me.
I could only shudder and shake.
I knew my dreams were a lie
and that I was a fake.

Running was useless
in hiding I would be found.
The chains were making me weary
I was so tightly bound!

I could continue no more
I was far too weak.
My present life was worthless.
My future looked bleak.

When I could walk no further
I began to crawl.
Broken and bleeding
I began to call.

I cried out in agony
I screamed your name
I was filthy clad in rags
I was full anguish and shame

When you came to me
I was afraid to look upon your face.
I was broken and worthless
yet you extended me grace.

This mask of clay
fell to the ground and was broken.
No longer hiding behind pretense
I listened to the words that were spoken.

You showed me your deep love.
You showed me that tree.
With a heart that was broken
I knew your sacrifice for me.

Without my mask
apparent was my broken soul.
You gathered the pieces of me;
replaced them to make me whole.

On this day of reckoning
I gave you all that was me.
I traded it for your love
And finally knew I was free.

The American dream is just that, a dream. The news and tabloids are full of the lies. We chase wealth only to find it is never enough. We seek beauty but hate what we see in the mirror. We lust for excitement yet become desensitized to nearly every experience. We seek love through a self need only to find ourselves deflated and alone. I know these things because I have been there. The lies of our enemy seem like goals worth pursuing. However, if there is any truth in them, why do we see the rich, famous and beautiful people in our culture dying of misery? Did they not have goals that brought them everything they thought they wanted? What happened when they got it all? Jesus gives us wise advice in John 12:24-25 when he says, "Listen carefully: Unless a grain of wheat is buried in the ground, dead to the world, it is never any more than a grain of wheat. But if it is buried, it sprouts and reproduces itself many times over. In the same way, anyone who holds on to life just as it is destroys that life. But if you let it go, reckless in your love, you'll have it forever, real and eternal." I know these words are contrary to the ones we are taught. It's important to look at who speaks the words we heed. What are the motives behind the promises in the commercials we watch? Do Donald Trump and Mary Kay want a personal relationship with you?

Will you be stubborn in your self pursuits? Will you continue to seek everlasting peace and joy in the shifting sands of our culture? You don't have to! There is another way. Lay the burdens of these cultural lies at the feet of our Master and trade them for life more abundant!

Does this sound like the longing of YOUR heart?

## *Distant Shores*

On this journey
I come to the edge of the sea.
Before me a tiny boat anchored
I step aboard
and pull the anchor free.

A small sail sits bunched
at the base of the mast.
Loosening it's tethering
I bid farewell
to all that has passed.

I know not where I'm going
but know precisely where
I have been.
This journey not so much
about distance covered
as what has happened within.

The sail fills with wind
and begins carrying me
far away from shore.
Awareness that not by
my own power do I travel.
On the other side
hopes of finding something more.

Hours turn into days
with the wind determining
my course and direction.
Suddenly my sail grows slack.
My heart fills with worry
and prayers for Your protection.

Here I sit
with nowhere I can go.
Oars in the hull of my boat
but my destination is far;
too far for me to row.

I know I should wait on You
Yet I am uncertain as to how.
If there was a time that I
needed You, my Lord
that time is now!

You are the wind in my sails
You are the voice that calms
the stormy sea.
It was Your voice
that opened the door of my prison.
It was Your voice that beckoned
setting this captive free.

Worry and panic return
and slowly grow into a deep fear.
"Send the northeasterly wind,"
I pray aloud
hoping You will hear.

The ruthless sun beats down
on this flat calm ocean.
Skin burns and throat parches.
No tears remain
to reveal my emotion.

When I think I can take no more
I spot storm clouds
gathering in the east.
I thank God in anticipation
of the rains
that soon will be released.

Waiting…
just a whisper of wind
comes and brings life to this sail.
It continues to build
gradually growing
to a full force gale.

Praising Your name
as I come to rest on the shores
of a far distant land.
Spreading good news to all
until those who accept it
are as numerous
as the grains of sand.


     Today's post is a continuation of Wednesday's. The first vision I was given on the morning of the 4th was of this seaward journey and His wind in my sails. Sometimes it's the flat calm amidst uncertainty that takes it's toll and the storm is what finally propels us forward. So if you are waiting for the wind to fill your sails this morning, I suggest that you pray to the One who brings the subtle breezes and the full force gales. His name is Jesus. He is my

## Doubt

When my heart grows cold
and the future looks bleak.
When a lasting peace
Is all that I seek.

When I am confused
and shaken to the core.
When my need for mercy
is met by a slamming door.

When I have no place to turn
and nowhere to confide.
When fear grips me deeply
and I have nowhere to hide.

When all that is within me
is tattered and torn.
When even my home
is a place that is foreign.

When my dreams are barren
in a land laid to waste.
When my hope is gone
and my mind is erased.

When I cry out for the rocks
to cover up my shame.
When I want to run away
and even deny my name.

When I look into the mirror
to see shattered pieces of my life.
When pain courses through me
until it cuts like a knife.

When I ponder this I wonder
is it still for me that you came?
When I know I am not worthy
for you to take my blame?

When I look at myself honestly I sometimes see some
terrible things. I have a past to be ashamed of. I have a present that
often seems meaningless and futile. I have a future on this earth
that is uncertain. I begin to turn introspective. I examine every
nook and cranny of my life. The deeper I look into my own heart,
the greater the depths of my despair. This condition we live in,
sin, can drag me down. At what point did I think I would become
immune to it? All of our pain is either the result of our own sinful
actions or of someone else's. No wonder it leads to our death! I'm
not referring to the death of our body, which we seem to fear all
too much, but in our spirit. In Romans 6: 22-23 we hear about our
new relationship to this sin nature. *"But now that you've found
you don't have to listen to sin tell you what to do, and have discov-
ered the delight of listening to God telling you, what a surprise! A
whole, healed, put-together life right now, with more and more of
life on the way! Work hard for sin your whole life and your pension
is death. But God's gift is real life, eternal life, delivered by Jesus,
our Master."*

What separates us from the suffering we endured at the
hands of sin? The most tremendous sacrifice that mankind has ever
witnessed! I will never feel worthy. I will never be worthy. This
is the nature of love. Jesus died for our sins. We have NOTHING
to offer in return. No matter how much we may choose to strive
as though we could offer something, it all pales in the face of his
completely unselfish love. Have you accepted this unselfish gift?

## *Drowning*

Stepping from the shore
I first enter the sea.
I barely notice the chains
that are wrapped tightly around me.

Up to my knees;
all appears to be well.
Even if I were hurting
no one could ever tell.

Up to my waist;
now a little more than I can bear.
My steps are slower now
I wonder how I will fare.

Up to my chest;
The chains weigh me down.
If the water gets much higher
I know that I will drown.

Up to my neck
And I am crying for assistance.
I can barely stay afloat
with all of this resistance.

Now I am in too deep.
I am in over my head.
If help doesn't come soon
I am sure to be dead.

If I could only escape the chains
I would never wear them again.
If I could only be free
From the weight of my sin!

Above I see a hand
reaching out to me.
It is the only chance remaining
to escape from the sea.

I reach as far as I can
I can hold my breath no more.
He grasps me firmly
pulling me to shore.

Taking my first breath of air
I feel much lighter than before
My chains stayed behind in the depths
And I sit upon the shore.

Looking up, a shadow in the sun
my savior smiles from above
He loosed the chains that bind
and replaced them with his love!


When I first entered the world of willful sin it was exciting. I wasn't willing to submit myself to restrictions. I wanted to do what I wanted to do! It was fun splashing around in the forbidden waters. Each step that I took brought me just a little deeper. I wasn't concerned. I had no outside perspective so everything seemed fine. The weight slowly weakened me. I wanted to walk back out of this sea of my sin but with the load I was carrying it was far easier to continue heading down hill into the depths. I was in real trouble but didn't have the foresight to call for help. Sure I had those moments where I sought to be quickly bailed out but each time help arrived, I let go of the lifeline. We commonly call this denial. My denial of my sin was threatening to kill me!

This is the reality of our sin. The wages are death. I was a dead man walking. I began to try to free myself of these self imposed chains, but I wasn't able to. They were wrapped tightly around me and locked with a key I didn't have. It was only when I began drowning that I cried out for a savior. I deserved to reap what I had sown. He could have left me there, but he was faithful to grab my hand and pull me from the sea. He unlocked the chains and left them in the depths. Do you feel the weight of your sin? Is it bearing down on you? Are you struggling for air? You can't free yourself from the chains but our Lord Jesus can. Cry out his name and I promise he will reach for you. Once you are in his grasp he will not let go!

## Earning Your Love

I carefully aimed for the target
but woefully missed my mark.
Moving without your guidance
is like a total shot in the dark.

I look at the squares surrounding
as I carefully consider my next move.
I step forward aggressively
as though I have something to prove.

Why do I strive so hard
for something that cannot be earned?
My works are like filthy rags.
In the end they will be burned.

Yet the burden of guilt and shame
hangs around my neck like a millstone.
The only way to relieve the weight
is found when I remain prone.

So I am caught in the middle
between the truth and a lie.
I find myself wedged in tightly
the more that I try.

I wish to escape this cruel place
I wish to live only within your grace.
My arms are stretched out wide
seeking the warmth of your embrace.

Am I worthy of your affections?
Can you truly love me just as I am?
My desire pours right over the top
as I crumble like a broken dam.

I feel so soiled in my shame.
I feel like I am not nearly enough.
Although I pretend that all is well
it's nothing more than a bluff.

Why would you choose to love
a wretch like me?
Why would you pay such a price
to set me free?

If you were raised in a home like mine you likely learned performance based love. I spent years in my youth striving to be enough. When I failed to measure up to the standards which were set, I would simply give up. I was a rebellious child to my parents and I have been a rebellious child to my heavenly Father. Yet as I find myself striving for some invisible standard to please him I realize that I will NEVER be enough. There is nothing I can do which measures up to God's perfect standard. More importantly, I have to remember that I am not loved for what I have or have not accomplished. I am loved because of the perfect gift given to me well before my birth. We are loved not because of what we have done, but because of what HE did for us!

Do you find yourself striving? Do you feel unworthy of God's love just as you are? Do you find yourself trying to change your behaviors in order to be more acceptable?

## End Of My Rope

Eyes open, eyes shut;
no difference on this dark night.
Stumbling in pitch blackness;
hoping only for the light.
Reaching out a hand;
attempting to feel the way.
Demons creep in quietly.
Swooping in to snatch peace;
holding my heart at bay.

The walls surround,
the floor beneath,
scattered shards of broken glass.
Hands and feet bare and bloodied,
My shame stands guard the exit,
demanding that none shall pass.

All that I own I barter
for some measure of peace.
Dare not negotiate freedom
The price too great
for my release.

Others share this space,
although their faces are
hidden from sight.
Like me,
they have scoured every corner.
Like me,
they have given up the fight.

A shrill scream
echoes through the darkness.
Cries of others lost soon follow.
Parting cracked, parched lips
The sound comes only as a whisper.
This voice seems so hollow.

Surely some light would reveal
the state of my affliction.
Surely some real love would mend
the brokenness of my addiction.
Yet who would wish to listen
to this poor, pathetic soul?
Who would extend mercy and grace
to make what is broken
complete and whole?

The abyss all that I see
when eyes are closed.
My own thoughts and words
reinforce guilt.
Shame silences my tongue
so that nothing is heard.

So not a sound is uttered
and I dare not hope.
Below lies utter destruction.
Growing weary of grasping;
reaching the end of my rope.

With the inevitable looming
Blistered hands
finally let go.
Gravity tugs mightily
as I fall
not knowing what's below.
These screams, my last…

Arms of love
up from beneath
halting an abrupt fall.
Arms of love
Surrounded then and there
answering a desperate call.

For I am not right
because any action of my own.
I am rescued wounded
from the darkness.
Now finally home.

## Faith in the One Unseen

Alone in a small restaurant
he eats with eyes that face down.
Evading the knowing glances of strangers
if he were to look up and around.

He returns to a dark apartment
where he sits all alone.
This is where he lays his head
but inside he longs for home.

No messages on his machine.
No word from those he holds dear.
He hates this void of silence.
It grips him with fear.

Slumping into the corner
sadness grips his heart.
The emptiness of his life
is slowly tearing him apart.

No comfort in laying his head down.
No peace to be found in sleep.
His eyes shutter as he sees the cliff;
envisions a fall so steep.

Tossing and turning
he is restless in his bed.
Looking to the stand beside him
he sees the bible by his head.

He had read this book before.
He knew many of the words.
He had prayed with clasped hands
but he wondered if anyone heard.

The mask is so heavy.
It's hard to hide all the pain.
Outside smiles and sunshine;
inside it's pouring rain.

He knew his future
and the result of status quo.
Could he replace this certain hell
for something he didn't know?

Now in total desperation
he falls to bended knee.
Willing to take the risk of prayer
to a God he couldn't see.

Now the rain from the inside
comes out in salty tears.
Trading in his self protection for trust;
a rock shatters his smoke and mirrors.

This God that evaded the eye
now touched his very soul.
He had risen today a broken man
but before bed he was made whole!

Do you ever find yourself hiding behind a mask? Are you scared to reveal what's really on the inside? It may seem like a gamble to drop the façade. After all, what if you revealed yourself and found rejection? The costs may seem too great. The fear of rejection is powerful. Yet, have you ever been in room full of people and still felt uncomfortable and alone? The fear is so powerful that many of us choose silent misery over the chance at real freedom! The cliff looms in front of you and it seems like a long way down. There is only one way you will find the strength to leave solid footing for uncertainty. Will you take that leap of faith?

## Falling down

When the mind grows numb
and my heart grows cold.
When I feel myself slipping
and cannot find a handhold.

When I put on a mask
to hide my real face.
When on the inside
I feel shame and disgrace.

When my bag of bones
seems to sag around me.
When I look in the mirror
and hate everything I see.

When I struggle to get out of bed
just to face another empty day.
When I seek your face
but feel you pulling away.

When each new day
seems just like the last.
When the quicksand sucks at me
and I find myself sinking fast.

When my eyes see blackness
and the chains wrap around me tight.
When I struggle against these burdens
and it seems like I am losing the fight.

When I run so fast
but find that I am going nowhere.
When I hear the pain of others
and find no reason to care.

When I trudge head down
but I should skip and run.
When I give up the battle as lost
yet you have already won.

When my burdens weigh so heavy
that I can hardly bare.
When I fall to my knees to seek you
but can't feel you in my prayer.

When the pallet of colors are gone
and all I can see is gray.
When my words seem so empty
that even I don't believe what I say.

Hollow, broken, empty, sullen, lost
I throw myself before your throne.
Saddened, disgraced, numb, burdened
I cannot face these things alone!

When oh Lord, my King,
will you hear my cries?
When will you give me courage
to discard my disguise?


    We all face struggles. Whether we know the Lord or not is inconsequential in this matter. Matthew 5:45 says … *"He causes his sun to rise on the evil and the good, and sends rain on the righteous and the unrighteous."* That's where the similarities end between those who believe and those who don't. When we have a personal relationship with Jesus we have a place to go. Sometimes we FEEL like we are alone, but we never are. Who will you call out to when you are struggling? Will you face your pain alone or will you call out HIS name? He is waiting for your cries. He is waiting for your HEART! You don't have to face this harsh and cruel world alone. Jesus tells us in John 16:33 … *"In this world you will have trouble. But take heart! I have overcome the world."* If you feel that this world has beaten you; if you believe your life lacks hope; turn it over to him now.

## Fill Me

I am a well
I am deep and I am wide.
The depths are filled with darkness
I am empty inside.

In this dry and parched place
I offer no life to those who thirst.
Those who drop their bucket into me
find only the worst.

My walls are cracked
The crevices are filled with dirt.
Without cleansing waters
I am left with only this hurt.

I pray earnestly for the rains
that will fill me from bottom to top.
I await an answer patiently;
but not a single drop.

So I will wait.
Right here will I stay.
Through the darkness of night;
on through the heat of the day.

I will watch each cloud
as it lazily drifts by.
I will hope in anxious anticipation
that one will eventually cry.

One day as I continued waiting
within my deepest parts a crack formed.
I felt cool waters bubbling.
But looking to the sky could see no storm.

It was in my broken state
and through my damaged heart
that life water entered in
just as I was coming apart.

I could feel it continuing forth.
The waters were beginning to rise.
It filled in the cracks of my walls
covering up all of the lies.

Nothing slowed the water's flow
as it continued towards the top.
It rejuvenated my broken places.
I prayed it would never stop.

Over the top it flowed
pouring out onto dry earth.
It was only a short time after
I bore witness to new birth.

Flowers sprang forth
from what was once just sand.
New life was springing up
throughout the land.


We are all wells. Without water we are just deep, dark holes in the ground. With water, we become a source of life. Creatures in the desert will travel from far around to reach such places. They will drink the life giving water. They will feed on the nourishment that becomes plentiful on the surrounding ground. A well that flows over positively affects everything around it.

What do you think of when you read this? What's the state of your well?

## *Finding Grace*

The church bells rang
in the tower across from her home.
She could see all the people there
yet here she was all alone.

Today she decided to join in.
She decided to enter into this place.
She snuck in as best she could
hoping no one would see her face.

On the back row she sat
as the people sang their songs.
They sang of the amazing grace
for which she had always longed.

She thought of the irony;
after all her name was Grace.
Yet she knew nothing of the meaning
and doubted she would find it in this place.

Many of them wore broad smiles
But her face still spoke of pain.
She had been to churches before
and swore she never would again.

Yet she wondered silently to herself
Was there really something to this Jesus?
Did he really love her as much as they say?
Is he really the god who sees us?

The preacher rose and spoke eloquently
as he began to talk about the topic of sin.
She considered her battle to do "right."
It seemed like one that she could not win.

But this preacher spoke of grace again
as he said, "Sin doesn't stand a chance
in competition with the forgiveness in grace!"
The words pierced her heart like a lance.

Could it be that His forgiveness
didn't depend on her ability to use willpower?
Could his love see beyond her sins
so she would no longer have to cower?

An invitation followed the sermon that day.
The tears began to well in her eyes.
Could she be bold enough to believe?
Was she willing to let go of all the lies?

She didn't come forward that day
She didn't even leave her seat.
But she began to cry out for forgiveness
As she found her knees and lost her feet.

The truth became evident to her
as she felt His Spirit well up inside.
He understood all of her sin and pain.
No longer would she need to hide!

The broken became whole on that day
The captives were set free.
Her mourning was turned to rejoicing.
She now understood his sacrifice on that tree!


        I want to speak clearly this morning. I know the lies. I
believed them for many years. I also know the truth of grace. As
human beings, we have a hard time with the concept. We want to
believe that "good" people somehow earn salvation while those
of us who are soiled are doomed to suffer the consequences of

our choices. Let me emphasize something. That is a LIE! I don't care who you are or what you have done; God's grace is greater than your sin! I have witnessed his grace firsthand, not only in my life, but in the lives of many others as well. Your shame tells you that you are beyond forgiveness. It tells you that you've committed offenses that have caused God to reject you forever. Again, let me say... LIE! I'm not talking theory here. I am talking about the story of my life. I am talking about a 38 year pursuit of all that I thought I wanted. I'm talking about a person who sometimes lived life without conscience. More importantly, I am talking about a person who now knows of his grace from personal experience. Let me assure you, if his grace is enough for me, it is more than enough for you!

Now that you know the truth what will you do with it? Will you consider all of the ways you have failed and decide you are beyond forgiveness? Perhaps you will choose to listen to my words. Perhaps you too will find grace. The word says "seek and you will find."

Does this state the desire of your heart? Do you wish to be free from this fear and shame?

## *For the Least of These*

Cars and people racing down the street;
a mass of metal and humanity.
Yet through all of this racing about
no one wants to stop and truly see.

We console ourselves when we are all alone
saying that "someday" we'll get it right.
We'll start living for something greater
before entering that last time into the night.

Until that time comes
with amassing we become occupied.
Always wishing that we had "more"
and yet never feeling quite gratified.

We don't see the man on the street corner
who is simply trying to get through the day.
We blind ourselves to the great need of this world
as we hurriedly scurry away.

We forget about the hungry
as we push their needs to the back of our minds.
We replace our thoughts and concerns for them
for all the wealth and gratification we can find.

For those who are thirsty
we give a never ending wait at the well.
Their souls long for the living water.
In withholding we leave them to hell.

Unsheltered beneath a noisy underpass
the homeless man lays alone.
While we desire a more extravagant house
he is simply looking for a place to call home.

For those who lack clothing;
who is out shivering in the cold.
Life has shown them no hint of mercy
whether they are young or they are old.

For that young girl laying in a hospital bed;
simply desiring to experience good health.
None of her treasures lie in what can be bought.
She is not in pursuit of any monetary wealth.

For the old man behind prison bars;
his one big mistake has cost him all these years.
He still lies awake at night dreaming of freedom.
He still fights back the tears.

Who are all of these people
and what do they mean to us anyway?
We put on the blinders to our world
and choose to trudge through another day.

So while the hungry go on starving;
while the thirsty whither to dust;
while the naked continue to shiver in the cold;
we pursue all of the treasures that will rust.

      The words I wrote above convicted me. To be honest, I am often one of those people who have the blinders on. Yet the need in our world is so great! The problems people face are not new and they are not isolated. They existed before our generation arrived and they will endure beyond our years on earth. Yet we sometimes seem content to offload these problems to our politicians and healthcare organizations. Who will stand up and make a difference? Who will feed the hungry? Who will provide clothing and shelter? I am SO selfish and it pierces me as I write these words. Below I want to share a portion of Matthew chapter 25, in a section commonly called "The Sheep and the Goats." I encourage you to read the entire passage. If my words and the words below tug at your heart, don't ignore them. We NEED leaders who will champion these causes. I will follow!

When he finally arrives, blazing in beauty and all his angels with him, the Son of Man will take his place on his glorious throne. Then all the nations will be arranged before him and he will sort the people out, much as a shepherd sorts out sheep and goats, putting sheep to his right and goats to his left.

"Then the King will say to those on his right, 'Enter, you who are blessed by my Father! Take what's coming to you in this kingdom. It's been ready for you since the world's foundation. And here's why:

I was hungry and you fed me,
I was thirsty and you gave me a drink,
I was homeless and you gave me a room,
I was shivering and you gave me clothes,
I was sick and you stopped to visit,
I was in prison and you came to me.'

"Then those 'sheep' are going to say, 'Master, what are you talking about? When did we ever see you hungry and feed you, thirsty and give you a drink? And when did we ever see you sick or in prison and come to you?' Then the King will say, 'I'm telling the solemn truth: Whenever you did one of these things to someone overlooked or ignored, that was me—you did it to me.'

So as the tears fill my eyes in conviction of my own selfishness, I will close. We are coming into the holiday season here in the U.S. with Thanksgiving and Christmas upon us. This is a time of real need for those who are suffering. Consider for yourself now, "How will I get involved and where can I make a difference?"

## Forever

Traveling this long road
there are a multitude of bends.
I cannot always see what lies ahead.
I know not where this journey ends.

So placing to worn paper
this weary and humble pen
there are only so many
things to say to you.
The most important among them
That LOVE WILL WIN.

He loved us first
before we even knew Him.
He is the light of the world.
Life without His love is dim.

He is the good shepherd
Who unconditionally loves His flock.
He stands before the door of our hearts
and behold it is He who knocks!

Don't deny His perfect love
Don't let this life slip away.
Don't put off until tomorrow
that which can be done today.

He already knows you are broken
and He loves you as you are.
He tends the sick and the wounded
He can even heal the scars.

His burden is easy and light
and we never carry it alone.
He even gave His son on a cross
so that you and I could be atoned.

Alpha and omega
Yet He knows our names.
Once we have experienced His love
we will never be the same.

We have never seen His face
Yet His creation cannot be
captured by the human eye.
He was. He is. He will be.
He rules the universe from
His throne on high.

He knows your name.
He knows your pain.
He loves you deeply.
He can break every chain.


There are not many words I can add to what is written above. I will say this; the Creator of the universe knows and loves you. He calls out to you and asks that you let Him come into your heart. He's not expecting that you "fix" yourself first. He isn't expecting that you put all of pieces back together. Let the One who knows you better than yourself do these things. He stands, not in front of you condemning, but beside you with His arm around your shoulder. Will you trust His deep and eternal love for you?

## Free

You came to walk
upon this barren land.
And in this place
you made your stand.

But to stand
you had to first fall.
You were not reluctant
To answer this call.

You humbled yourself
and paid for my sin.
You conquered in a battle
That I could not win.

I praise you today
for all that you have done.
For the victory in my heart
That you have won.

All of eternity
will echo with your name
With your perfect sacrifice
You took on my blame.

It was you
that captured my cold heart
It was you
that gave me a fresh start.

I want to shout from the mountains
I want to give all that I own
For yesterday I was in despair
but today I am not alone.

What is your name
the one that freed us?
I know your name well
your name is Jesus!

## *Healing Rain*

The palace is decorated in all its finery
And those who have gathered wear their best.
Wide smiles adorn so many faces
Small talk is exchanged between the guests.

I stand in the middle of this ballroom
My proximity to so many says I am not alone.
Yet I find myself longing to go deeper
I find myself longing to go home.

Hidden behind the walls of these smiles
They are dams designed to disguise the pain
Am I the only one who desires "real?"
Am I the only one who craves healing rain?

Turning in circles to look beyond
There is only this sea of faces.
Now I can see the charcoal pencil drawings
Each and every painted smile it traces.

Seeing beyond these facades of the front stage
The actors are practicing their lines.
If they knew of your wondrous love and grace
For your true freedom would they pine.

Yet we are all putting on performance
I am unwillingly drawn into this cast.
I put on my own pretentious smile
And I hope that I am able to last.

The effort of the act leaves me empty
the wine does not satisfy.
More than anything craving your living water
But in this desert I am dry.

The heaviness of my heart has me seeking you
For a moment a nod my head in prayer
Silently I scream your name at the top of my lungs
Hoping that you will be there.

Looking back across the crowded room
Something new comes to light.
A sign hangs around each neck
Making visible each person's plight.

Conversations shift from the pleasantries
There is nowhere left to hide.
These masks are worthless props
Now that each sign reveals what is inside.

Tears begin to fall like rain
As the hidden soul beneath is revealed.
These drops that fall are like summer showers
Give way to the true sunshine when we are healed.

People work hard at projecting to the world around them that they are all right. The vulnerability that goes along with showing anything otherwise is scary. What price do we pay for remaining hidden? The fact is we are never likely to receive magic glasses that show us the "real" that is hidden so carefully behind the mask, but what if we could? What if we could see what was really going on inside? Would we treat people differently or would we crush those glasses under foot and return to our ignorance?

God is the great lover of our souls. He is there to heal our deepest hurts when we trust him. However, I have found that he seldom works alone. We are meant to come along side of one another in our times of need. We were meant for true community. Have your magic glasses revealed someone who's hurting in your life? Now that you know about it, what will you do?

## Heaven's Manna

I am where I am in this great big world.
I am a creature of this land.
Yet no matter where I find myself
I know it was by the works of your hand.

A life of faith is not quite the same
when I have no great need.
No physical longing for sustenance
so I live a life without heed.

A life of greed was never your calling.
I have no need to hoard.
Yet I hold onto things I do not need
and strive for what I cannot afford.

If your manna fell from heaven
it would certainly go to waste on me.
Would I even recognize your provision
when I am so blind that I cannot see?

What an ungrateful wretch I am
when I don't look around and see
the abundance of blessings
that you have already provided to me!

So rather than thinking to myself "more"
what would happen if I gave it all away?
All of this still belongs to you
at the end of the day.

What if I treated everything as a gift from you
rather than the works of my own hand?
What if I build my home upon the rock
and moved away from these shifting sands?

Consumerism sounds like what it is
when it is what consumes.
Yet the lilies of the field don't worry
and look at the beauty when they bloom!

So may I praise you for your love.
May your name always be on my tongue.
May I scream of your mercy from the mountains
as long as breath fills these lungs!

May the gifts you have given me
Be found amongst these words.
May my voice not be alone in the desert
where it will not be heard.

 

      Here in the United States we are bombarded with marketing. We are told about all of the things we don't have that will bring us happiness. We are taught that "enough" is just a little more than what we have. It is so easy to be consumed by the allure of things. Yet if you are like me, you have earned your way to some of those goals to which you aspired only to find that the void was still there. The madness can perpetuate itself as we latch onto the next great desire. All of these shiny new things are destined for the rubbish heap. Our lives can very easily follow if we allow ourselves to be consumed by them. So what is worthy to occupy our minds and therefore our hearts? Paul puts it well in 1 Corinthians 13 when he says, *"Trust steadily in God, hope unswervingly, love extravagantly. And the best of the three is love."* Trust, hope and love; these are the things that will remain in the end. God won't ask us what kind of car we drove. He won't ask us about whether we lived in our dream home. He won't be concerned about whether we reached the level of greatness we sought in our careers. He will ask, "Did you trust ME?" "Did you hold out hope for the things I promise?" "Did you do as I said and love others?" I know that I will have many selfish ambitions to answer for on that day. Whatever you do, don't follow in my footsteps. Don't aspire to the things of this world. Instead, do as Jesus said in John 12: 24-25 *"...Unless a grain of wheat is buried in the ground, dead to the world, it is never any more than a grain of wheat. But if it is buried, it sprouts and reproduces itself many times over. In the same way, anyone who holds on to life just as it is destroys that life. But if you let it go, reckless in your love, you'll have it forever, real and eternal."*

## *His Name*

From the mouths of the saints
it is carried upon a delicate breeze.
Although he remains hidden to us
we know that he sees.

His heart is visible in our hearts.
His ways are visible in ours.
The strong winds of His change
have freed us from the prison bars.

Now with wide eyes of wonder
much more has come into sight.
We know he never leaves or forsakes.
He is not blind to the human plight.

Who shall compare to the beauty
found just in knowing his name?
He discovered us in dark alleyways
in His light we are never the same.

The broken are made whole.
The lost souls are finally found.
We worship His holy name in awe
as our faces find the ground.

So we come to the public streets
unable to stay silent about His grace.
The judge is pounding His gavel
"Not guilty!" the verdict on our case.

How could we still our tongues
after receiving such a marvelous gift?
We are anchored in the rock of truth.
No longer are we set adrift.

We were born once to this world
but our second birth brought us home.
We take our places at His table.
No longer will we be cursed to roam.

More will join in the celebration.
They will lay their burdens at his feet.
We will hold our arms high above
as we witness sin's final defeat.


      For those of us who have received God's grace there is much cause for celebration. Like the woman referenced in Luke chapter 7, I have been forgiven many, many sins. As a result I am very, very grateful! My forgiveness wasn't received because of who I am, but because of who HE is. So it's only natural that I wouldn't live my life out of who I think I am, but out of who HE says I am. I am righteous and holy, even on my worst day. I am not free from sin and pain but I am free of the long term consequences. The best part is that this forgiveness is extended to all who seek it. So why are you dragging your shame around behind you? Why are you allowing the things that you have done define you now? You are more than the sum total of your past actions. How do I know? I know because I have been there and I have done that. The day I cried out His name in anguish was the day that I was healed. This you can be sure of. You must ask to receive and you must seek to find. What are the desires of your heart?

## His Sacrifice

Standing in the arena
I feel the earth beneath my feet.
Blood of the unworthy has fallen.
The crowd is out of their seats.

They jeer and they shout.
They scream for my blood.
Their hatred penetrates my armor.
Their anger overcomes like a flood.

The lion faces me,
penetrating eyes beneath a matted mane
He seeks to destroy me.
He takes joy in my pain.

I see my life flash before me.
I am overcome with fear.
I see no escape from this judgment.
I realize that the end is near.

My eyes dart from side to side.
But there is nowhere to flee.
The crowd chants for death.
I fall to my knees.

Then I see a spotless lamb before me,
separating me from certain fate.
He draws my attention to an outlet
behind the cruel lion stands a gate.

The king of beasts roars
and is released from his chains
The lamb stands fearless before him
ready to take on my pain.

The lion's teeth dig deep
crimson red mingles with white.
It would seem the lamb is defenseless,
unable to win this fight.

I run quickly for my escape.
I am afraid to turn back and see
the lamb that gave his life
so that I might be free.

I reach the narrow gate
and turn back in a parting glance.
The lamb lay slain before the lion.
He never had a chance.

The lion had his blood
dripping from snarled jowls.
He begins to devour the lamb
And the crowd around him howls.

My heart races
nearly beating out of my chest
The mere fact that I am breathing
means surely that I am blessed.

The spotless lamb is worthy.
He has quenched their blood lust.
He laid down his life for me
And in him alone do I trust.


My words do not come easily this morning. I couldn't possibly do justice to the price that was paid for us. Jesus WILLINGLY laid down his life so that we could be freed from our sin debt. There was no one else that was worthy to be the sacrifice. I tend to glance over the details when I consider Christ's death.

There was so much more than a cross. Christ endured emotional pain and suffering well before he felt anything physical. He was rejected by his own people. They cried out for his blood. Even our worst serial killers haven't faced such physical torture. Before he even reached the cross he had been whipped nearly to death. He had been mocked and beaten. People spat in his face. Then in his weakened state he was forced to drag his own cross up the hill. He could have walked away at any point. He could have decided that it just wasn't worth it. If he had died that day and been placed in the tomb to rot and decay he would have been like any other man. He wasn't! On the third day he arose in victory. Even death couldn't conquer our king! Do you know sacrifice like this? Have you received this kind of love? Do you know the one who conquered the grave? His gift was given freely. Will you accept it?

## His Touch

The pain inside of me
just won't go away.
Every morning I wake with it
and it persists throughout the day.

I have seen the all of doctors
and spent everything that I possess.
Yet with all of their expertise
I am penniless and still can't find rest.

For twelve years this has persisted.
I would give anything to ease the pain.
Even looking up at a cloudless sky
all that I can see is rain.

Then I heard about this man.
He helps the deaf to hear.
He helps the blind to regain sight.
The lame stand up and walk without fear.

If only I could find this Jesus
that some say is son of the Most High.
I will give anything to see him;
just to have him walk by.

On this day a crowd approaches.
Excited people are running ahead.
They say that the rabbi, Jesus
is on his way to raise the dead!

This was the chance I waited for
but the crowd was pressing in.
I reached with all that I had in me
and was just able to touch his hem.

Instantly I felt the sickness leave me
and my sadness was taken away.
All of it was replaced with pure joy.
I would always remember this day!

But within a moment the Master stopped
and demanded to know who touched his robe.
No one owned up to his accusation
but he continued to probe.

With bended knees and trembling hands
I confess my whole story.
As I spoke and retold my life
I never realized it would be used for his glory.

When I finished he smiled and said,
"Daughter, you took a risk trusting me
now you're healed and whole."
Rejoicing, I went away... FREE!


This poem is inspired by real life events. The story was told in Luke Chapter 8: 40 – 48. There are a number of aspects to this, but for the point I would like to make, I want to focus on just one. Faith is a powerful thing! We are all broken inside and we all have a choice on whether we will simply make do or whether we will seek the hem of his robe. It was this woman's faith that healed her. For all I know there were others in that same crowd who also had ailments. They too may have touched Jesus. This woman who suffered so much wasn't healed because she touched Jesus. She was healed because she believed that by touching Jesus she would be. Depending on the version of the Bible you read this in, you may see the statement "your faith has healed you." However, in the message version, he says the words just as I placed them in the poem, "you took a risk in trusting me." I have just one question for you. Whether you are a believer or not, this question applies to you. Will you take a risk and trust him? Our bodies will all wear out and we will die. This is a fact that we can all be certain of. Yet the healing that Christ is ready to provide you isn't just for your body, which only here temporarily. It is for your soul, which will live on forever!

## *Home*

If you could open my chest;
if you could see all that is inside of me
You would find a heart beating
and a soul that longs to be free.

I have run so far away
I can hardly remember your face.
Yet as I sit here among the swine
I long for your warm embrace.

I think of the kindness in your eyes.
I recall the times that I leaned into you.
In those times of deepest turmoil
you have always been the one that is true.

I envision those times
when the sun filled the sky with light.
It is the recollection of those days
that keeps me sane in this night.

Although you seem so far away
my mind's eye sees you waiting patiently.
I can almost hear my name in the wind
as you continue softly calling to me.

May you be the compass
that leads me back to my true home.
Once I return to your arms of love
never again will I long to roam.

I have been a part of a lot of personal conversations. One of the most commonly asked questions I hear is "How could God possibly forgive me?" Sometimes it seems like we are beyond his grace. It seems like we have fallen so far that there is no hope of salvation. Yet these feelings are contrary to the truth. Although there are many scriptures that talk about forgiveness, this is a favorite of mine. It comes from Psalms 103. *"God is sheer mercy and grace; not easily angered, he's rich in love. He doesn't end-lessly nag and scold, nor hold grudges forever. He doesn't treat us as our sins deserve, nor pay us back in full for our wrongs. As high as heaven is over the earth, so strong is his love to those who fear him. And as far as sunrise is from sunset, he has separated us from our sins."*

Is your heart filled with grief over your past mistakes? Do you desire to be separated from these things? Repent and trust our Father at his word. As 1 John 1:9 says, *"If we admit our sins—make a clean breast of them—he won't let us down; he'll be true to himself. He'll forgive our sins and purge us of all wrongdoing."* So do you see him? Do you see him standing there calling your name? May he be the compass that leads you to your true home.

## Hope For the Hopeless

He stands beneath a busy underpass
while all the vehicles hurry by.
By no means is he alone in this hurried mass
yet the loneliness inside makes him start to cry.

Beside him his faithful companion;
clearly he shares in his master's pain.
His ribs show the signs of hunger
and his fur is infested with mange.

He doesn't know of the better times
and is satisfied with his human friend.
He's never given a thought to another.
He will be there until the end.

All of his master's possessions
fit into a single dingy pack.
All of the things he has remaining
he carries on his back.

There were no valuable treasures contained within
but to him these precious items have the worth of gold.
Mostly memories of better days passed
like props in stories waiting to be told.

There was that old book of matches
He had never struck a single one.
They advertise what was once his business
They only thing left when all was said and done.

The tattered baseball cards
with the names of heroes now returned to dust.
He kept them in an old tin can.
The years of moisture pocked the surface with rust.

An old piece of dried beef jerky
that he didn't know he would find.
He holds it out to his last remaining companion
and puts the pangs of hunger out of his mind.

Looking to the sky above him
he is met with a full view of gloom and gray.
The cold had fully penetrated
as he hadn't felt the warmth of sun in days.

Falling into a momentary trance
The cars continue to race by.
He had once been just like them
but now he just hoped to die.

Dark, foul emotions he could never escape
loomed deep within his soul.
Long ago he had given up hope of returning.
Long ago he had given up on being whole.

Time to trudge forward,
Time to make it through another day.
He never anticipated meeting another
as he traveled along the way.

Moving along with eyes cast down
He sees in his path the feet of another.
He looks up to see before him
someone watching with the loving eyes of a mother.

She held in her hands a small pack of her own
She had it far out in front of her as if offering.
Only this pack she held was new
And filled with many desirable things.

He sees the smile that crosses her face
as her lips parted to bring their first words.
As she spoke aloud to him
He couldn't believe what he heard.

"Sir, I thought of you
as I filled this bag full of things."
He reached out with a new hope
and the unanticipated joy that it brings.

Was it really possible
that someone out there would still care?
He had been so long alone and forgotten
love was not an option and he was caught unaware.

Momentarily he cast his eyes back down
As he looked to his faithful pal.
Dog smiles and tail wagging
replaced his normal scowl.

She noticed him too.
Without hesitation she reached out.
It was love at first pet
of this he had no doubt!

Again unanticipated kindness and love
as she said "Sir, I would like to feed and bathe your friend."
"I will be glad to give you a ride to somewhere
And my car is just around the bend"

Now there were tears again
But now they were tears of joy.
He reached back down to pat his dog
As he exclaimed, "Come on boy!"

As I think of this I am reminded of Matthew chapter 25 when Jesus tells the story about the sheep and the goats. I am not going to repeat it here, but I do want to mention it. The "goats" are the ones who were oblivious to their surroundings, or perhaps they simply didn't care. Much of my life has been spent as a goat. I was so preoccupied with getting what I thought I deserved that I didn't concern myself with the needs of others, particularly those who were commonly overlooked. Yet we are surrounded by the over-looked, the downtrodden, the broken, and the OUTSIDERS. I wonder, how was it possible for me to really not notice them? Yet if I open my eyes and look around I see him standing there on the street corner. I see him on the front steps of a run down building. I see him off in a dark corner trying not to be noticed. I encourage you NOT to be who I was. Don't be a goat. Give of yourself to others. Give generously and with a heart of love. That could be you standing there and it may be yet!

## The Lamb of Life

I walk...
dragging my feet as I go.
Smiling only half smiles
hoping the pain won't show.

I stand...
isolated and alone.
Hiding in dark corners
where my cover won't be blown.

I sit...
by myself with my fears.
Using pretense and masks
To hold back the tears.

I lay...
with troubling thoughts.
I wrestle them in futility
losing many battles fought.

I scream...
when the frustration becomes too great.
I fight what appears destiny
denying that it could be fate.

I cry...
feeling that it will always be the same.
Bowing my head,
I am isolated by shame.

I call...
upon the healer's name.
Praying for strength
knowing I will never be the same.

I trust...
the words that he brings.
Rebuking the tapes
that tells me these things.

## I Am "No One"

Who am I
to fight a war with a pen?
Engaging an unseen enemy;
am I in a battle I cannot win?

I find myself drifting
off into reflective thought.
I consider those won and lost
in the battle being fought.

You still love your children.
You stay true to your word.
May your seed find fertile soil
for all that have heard.

Yet I have failed;
I have fallen short in this goal.
Yet I continue to pray that we will find freedom.
I continue to pray that we will be made whole.

When it all seems futile
I find myself calling your name.
Even in the depths of my sorrow
You take away my shame.

You hear my cries when I call
You forgive me when I am weak.
You understand that even now
it is your face that I seek.

My name is "no one"
for I cannot provide the solution.
You are the true Master.
Only you can lead this love revolution.

May that person who is out there hurting
know that they are not alone.
May your whisper become a scream
as you call them home.

May the majesty of your voice be heard
from the top of the highest mountains.
Even clearer in the depths of the valley;
may your grace be our eternal fountain.

May we all become divine "nobodies"
May we all point the way to grace.
May each person who looks to find you
See for themselves your true face.


      For all of my talk about grace I hate my mistakes. I hate
my failures! Yet when I fail I realize I have a choice. I can choose
to wallow in my mistakes. I can allow myself to become my own
worst accuser or I can choose to rely on grace. I am reminded that
when I first started writing I had a vision. I could see myself lying
flat on the ground. I realize that I am truly no one. That may sound
like I am really down on myself, but it's quite the contrary. I am no
one, but I know the one great Someone. For that matter I know the
great Someone who is EVERYTHING. May I assume and main-
tain my prone position; the position of a servant. May you find that
you hardly even notice me, but you see HIM clearly. His name is
Jesus and he is calling your name. He is calling you home. May his
whisper become a scream in your life.

## Idols of Babylon

The statue of gold is erected
and we the people are bound.
When the band strikes up in chorus
we are to fall to the ground.

But I only serve one God
and he is not made of gold.
I will not bow down before another
even in fear of death I will not fold.

So when the big band plays
I will raise my hands to my Lord.
He is the only king of my heart
who's grace I cannot even afford.

So heat up your fires, oh king
and prepare to throw me in.
Even if I am consumed by them
in the end I know who will win!

I believe in the power my God.
I have faith that he will deliver me.
No ropes can bind my soul.
Inside I know that I am free!

Into the fires I am cast
and my faith is put to the test.
But I am unscathed by them;
proving that by HIM I am blessed.

So call me out now king of men
so that with your eyes you can see.
No fire will consume my flesh
and you too must agree.

The King of kings will call
all of us together in the end.
Then every tongue will confess
and every single knee will bend.

So when this promised day arrives
you can be sure that I will bow!
But today is not that day
and no other gods will he allow!

(Inspired by Daniel Chapter 3)


There aren't any golden statues here in the United States that were made to be worshipped. Yet, we don't need them. Idols abound in the land of the free. We are bombarded by media, surrounded with entertainment options, hit hard by sex and pornography, vanity, alcohol, drugs, cars, houses, careers... The list goes on and on. All of these are things that we can potentially find ourselves bowing down to. Yet we are loved by one God... THE one God. He didn't want his people worshipping golden statues then and he sure doesn't want us bowing before the many idols of the modern world. We are given a choice as to who we wish to worship and serve. I suggest that we choose wisely! Do you find yourself distracted by the idols of this world? Have they captured your mind and your heart? Yet with all of these distractions, do you find yourself with an empty hole inside of you that you can't explain? I know the One who can fill it and I would be glad to help you in the introductions!

## *Illusions of the Dark*

Early in the morning
I stumble with little use of sight.
Although I know the morning is coming
I still face the darkness of night.

Unable to continue further
I stop and rest along the way.
I wonder at the stars and their beauty
yet I long for the light of day.

Struggling to grasp my surroundings
shapes become monsters of the black.
They hide their true identities in this shroud
ready to lunge forward for the attack.

My heart rate quickens
as I am unable to discern friend from foe
Running from them is futile
the darkness will follow wherever I go.

The coyotes sing in the distance
Their lonely howls penetrate my soul.
I am dreadfully alone in this place
with no one there to console.

I am transformed into a small child.
I am truly afraid of the night.
There is no rescue from this prison;
save the day's first light.

As I peer around me
these looming shapes begin a transformation.
The first appearance of the sun
pierces the darkness bringing promise of salvation.

The sinister shapes of the darkness
begin to reveal themselves under the power of light.
Ultimately they could not hide forever
under the concealment of the night.

I thank my Lord for his deliverance
and for bringing to me his Son.
He delivered me from this darkness
when I had no place to run.


    Darkness is tricky. It is deceptive. It can make monsters out the benign and make that which truly means to do us harm look harmless. We do our best to discern our surroundings when consumed by night but our eyes are rendered useless by sheer lack of light. Such is the world of sin. Maybe it starts out in the light of day but it slowly transforms into evening. As the even the shadows fade and we are enveloped by the blackness of night we don't initially realize our predicament. Then it sinks in. We are alone in the dark! Although the various stages day and night are unchanging realities in the physical world, there is no requirement for darkness in our spiritual world. God sent his only Son to die for us so we would no longer need to stumble around in the dark. We don't need to fear the looming shapes of sin. They are conquered by His perfect love and grace!

    Are you stumbling in the darkness? Are the shapes that surround you playing games with your mind? Jesus said in John 11: 9-10 *"Are there not twelve hours of daylight? Anyone who walks in daylight doesn't stumble because there's plenty of light from the sun. Walking at night, he might very well stumble because he can't see where he's going."*

    If you are beaten and bruised by sin maybe it's time you stop stumbling through the dark. Maybe it's time to find your knees instead and pray for the light of HIS day.

## In My Skin

I open my eyes.
A new day begins.
Another day in my life;
another day in my skin.

I find myself wondering
What if I awakened in another place?
What if I was in someone else's skin?
Would I still see your face?

What if I was hungry?
What if I was in need?
What if I suffered
while witnessing other's greed?

What would I know
if I were in another land?
Would I acknowledge your love?
Would I see the works of your hand?

What if me was not me
and I did not know the things I do now?
Would you still find a way to reach me
Would you still show me your love somehow?

So if me were not me
would there be another me reaching out?
Would there be another me
to show me what Jesus is about?

If me were not me;
would someone be there to love me?
If me were not me;
would I still know who can set me free?

Who will reach out to me?
Who will give me a drink when I thirst?
Who will feed my soul
if this very day were my worst?

Oh how my heart desires
to reach out beyond the world I see!
Oh how your heart desires
to set ALL of the captives free!

I close my eyes.
Another day ends.
Another day in my life;
another day in my skin.


　　　Webster's dictionary defines empathy as "the intellectual iden-
tification with or vicarious experiencing of the feelings, thoughts,
or attitudes of another". It's a word that we hear often yet I would
challenge how often we actually utilize the concept itself in our
own lives. There is a great big world around us and its full of
people. Each of them brings unique experiences and backgrounds
into the mix. Yet for all of our differences we have common ground.
We have a need for food. We have a need for clean water to drink.
We have a need to experience unconditional love. We have a need
to experience true forgiveness. We have a need for a Savior! If you
were not you, who would be out there reaching out to you now?
Wouldn't you still want someone to meet your needs?

## In the Grasp of the Enemy

Standing in this valley of darkness
I feel vulnerable and alone.
I am overcome with sadness.
More than anything, I long for home.

In the distance a cloud of dust;
the enemy approaches fast.
All of my days leading to this one
Now I am hoping this won't be my last!

My adversary comes before me;
with chariots guided by dark knights
I stand alone, surrounded
Who will join me in this fight?

Horses lathered with sweat
Draw close with nostrils flared.
The stench of death and decay
permeates the inky air.

Now arrows of accusations fly
loosed by hands determined to destroy.
Without your shield I am vulnerable
and will fall beneath their evil ploy.

Now swords from scabbards drawn;
the ground shakes as they draw near.
My eyes are assaulted by their numbers
and I am overwhelmed with fear.

They are given to their anger
with souls of wormwood.
Would strike the life out of me
if they only could.

Alone I know I stand no chance
and cry out to be delivered by my King.
I pray for his army of justice.
I anticipate the victory they bring.

I turn my eyes to the hills
And spy an army of sheer light.
Brighter than the sun
I must shield them from my sight.

The lions come forward to devour me.
But now their mouths are bound tight.
Without deadly blood soaked fangs to bear
they have lost their will to fight.

They turn tail and run,
Shrill screams as they fade away.
The blindness of their night
is replaced by light of day.


Sometimes it seems like I am fighting a battle that I can't
win. Ephesians 6: 10-12 tells us *"God is strong, and he wants you
strong. So take everything the Master has set out for you, well-
made weapons of the best materials. And put them to use so you
will be able to stand up to everything the Devil throws your way.
This is no afternoon athletic contest that we'll walk away from and
forget about in a couple of hours. This is for keeps, a life-or-death
fight to the finish against the Devil and all his angels."* So, alone,
I am destined to lose! I am destined to repeat the same mistakes.
I am destined to fall to temptation. But the truth is that I am not
alone unless I choose to be! God promised the he would never
leave us or forsake us. So with him on my side, the battle is already
won!

Are you fighting a losing battle? Do you look your opponents in the eye and shutter with fear? The odds are impossible when we face them alone but victory is assured when he is by our side! Will you call HIM to join you on your own personal battlefield?

## *In The Moment*

As I look to the picture on my wall
sadness invades my heart.
I see those I have loved and lost.
Grief reaches from deep within
and threatens to tear me apart.
I ask the futile question, "Why?"
but know the answer won't be found.
I see images before me
yet cannot turn back time's hand.
It slips out from beneath me
like tiny grains of sand.
Oh, to regain what was lost
on this long and tiresome journey.
I would pay any cost
to have them returned to me.
If only for a single day;
if only for a moment in time.
To hold them again in my arms;
to know that they are okay.
But not all has been lost.
My Creator has a perfect plan.
When I feel alone in my grief
I open the eyes of my heart
and find he is holding my hand.
Even my loneliness does not separate;
even my doubt does not set us apart.
On that day that I said, "yes"
He came to live in my heart.
I compare this to the losses
and know that more has been gained.
For I stand a free man now
when once I was chained.
So I praise Him for His mercy
and trust Him through both gain and loss.
I need only see that tree;
to know he will pay any cost.

## In the Presence of the King

I see the waning of the moon
before the dawn of the day.
I cannot wait for the sun to come
and chase the night away.

Over the horizon the dawn's first light;
a brilliant array of color and hue.
I am in awe of it's sheer beauty
Another day has dawned anew.

I peer off into the eastern sky
shielding my eyes from the light.
It's illumination is pure and true.
Nothing is hidden, all is in sight.

Dropping to my knees
I gaze upon your face.
Pure light and love surround me
as you show yourself in this place.

For a moment I feel unworthy
as my shame begins pulling me away.
Still I see the smile upon your face
I hear you urge me to stay.

Trusting your assessment over my own
I continue to look upon you, my Lord.
No price I could pay would buy your love
You are so much more than I can afford!

Yet no price was paid of my own doing
It was all taken care of in advance.
As you suffered and died upon that tree
and your side was pierced with the lance.

A vision seared into my mind
as I saw you hanging there all alone.
The pain of betrayal broke your heart
yet for my sins did you atone.

Tears of joy and pain well from within.
Now they begin down my cheeks.
All the answers I looked for on my own
were in the only place I did not seek.

Hands now reach into the sky
as I sing and praise your holy name.
I can no longer remain silent
because I will never be the same!

For me there is no doubt, once we have experienced God's perfect love, it changes us forever. The exact manifestation for each person is different but there is common ground. I am insanely grateful for the fact that God would even love someone like me but the truth is that he does! As I mentioned a few weeks ago, Jesus made his position loud in clear when he said, "I came for the sin sick, not the spiritually fit." Initially I cursed God for making me "sin sick." Now I praise him for it! The reality is that we are all sick yet only some of us realize it. It's in this awareness of our sickness that we seek a physician. He wants us all to be well. He wants us all to be whole and healed. So many of us continue to rely on ourselves and our own strength to make it through but it doesn't have to be this way. Matthew 11: 28-30, Jesus says, *"Are you tired? Worn out? Burned out on religion? Come to me. Get away with me and you'll recover your life. I'll show you how to take a real rest. Walk with me and work with me—watch how I do it. Learn the unforced rhythms of grace. I won't lay anything heavy or ill-fitting on you. Keep company with me and you'll learn to live freely and lightly."* Maybe this promise sounds too good be true, but it is true. How do I know? I live in this promise today! It's not because of who I am. It's about who HE is.

Feeling weary? Maybe you are worn down and uncertain how you will continue on. Maybe you are emotionally frazzled to the point where you can't take anymore. You will reach this place many times in your life, my friend. Yet each time you find yourself here you will have choice. Will you carry your burden or lay it down before the King?

## In the Shadows

I stand in the shadows
where I can be tucked far away.
The unknowns of darkness unsettling
Yet I also fear the light of day.

I wear my mask and my hood.
They veil me in protection.
Yet I am unreachable, untouchable;
unable to receive true affection.

These shadows were so broad.
in the beginning of the day.
But now as my life wears on
I see them slowly slipping away.

With each passing hour
my dread of exposure increases.
My mind is completely consumed
so that the terror never ceases.

Please don't cast me into the darkness!
Please don't make me face the light!
I prefer the shadows of gray
To the utter darkness of night!

But in these shadows I cannot walk freely
I am a captive left to hide.
If only someone would take my hand;
face the light of judgment by my side.

I could finally walk in the open
where I would be truly free.
My mask and hood cast aside
so that all would look upon the real me.

Yet as I stand here with arms crossed
people continue to stream right by.
Does no one see me in this limbo?
I fear that in this state I will die!

Among all of the hurriedness of this world
One stops and reaches out his hand.
He whispers to me so softly
promising to lead me out unto this land.

My hesitation is short lived
As I consider my last remaining choice.
I reach out my hand to grasp his,
responding now to the sound of his voice.

I step out of the shadows after years
And now it is all clear under the Son.
He loved me even while I was in hiding
And now there is no need to run.

I am all too familiar with the shadows. Much of my life I spent hiding in them. On one hand I was a "good upstanding Christian" but that was only my public face. Behind the scenes I found the person that I knew myself to truly be. When the mask came off I was faced with my true self. This person didn't resemble the one that I acted out before the rest of the world. Hidden from all of them was my shame, my disgust and self loathing. I feared that coming out of the shadows into the light would ultimately result in rejection. I believed that the love I received from the community around me was conditioned on being this person that I thought they wanted to see. Meanwhile the shadows weighed heavily on me. They drained me of my spiritual and emotional life blood. I longed for freedom! I wanted to show the person that I had hidden from the world. God knew this person all along and yet HE still loved me. Why couldn't the same apply to people?

Are you hiding in the shadows? Does your mask afford you the protection that you desire? Do you find yourself wondering what it would be like to take the mask away and reveal the real you? Take it from me, one who has been there and done that, you will never find freedom until you do! God has loved you all along. He sent his son to die for us while we were still sinners. What greater love is there?

## Encounter With Jesus

Eyes slowly open.
Feet hit the floor.
Another day begins this way;
just as thousands had before.

The desire for this new day
simply was not there.
It was not for a lack of searching.
He had looked everywhere.

Lasting peace and satisfaction
weren't found in things he acquired.
He searched his heart honestly
but couldn't find much to be admired.

As the streams of water poured
they mixed with salty tears.
Pain mingled with sorrow
along with his many fears.

Never would he be enough
Never would he be whole.
All the cracks in this vessel
kept it from ever being full.

Oh how he longed to break away;
to discover a place that is free.
He was a prisoner to his own life
and to the lock there was no key.

"What is this life for?"
"What is my purpose?"
The questions went deep;
well beyond the surface.

Out of the shower
he began drying with a towel.
The mood that took grip of him
was self destructive and fowl.

Self hatred and shame
were familiar territory for him.
Another day in this pit
and the light was growing dim.

Maybe he was better off dead.
Maybe there was no reason to exist.
He wondered if he should end it all.
He doubted he would be missed.

Out the door and into the car;
he began driving as he did each day.
The tears began to well up again
and he could not hold them at bay.

Pulling off to the side
as he found himself driving blind.
Head resting on the steering wheel
thinking about how life was unkind.

He couldn't stop the sobbing.
He couldn't regain his control.
All these years of wasted life
were beginning to take their toll.

"What about me?"
He knew this was not his thought.
He couldn't get past the question
no matter how much he fought.

Me was HIM
and he had known HIM before.
He had let HIM in once in life
before ultimately slamming the door.

"Would you take me back?"
The answer was a resounding "Yes!"
"Even after all that I have done?"
"I have so many things to confess!"

"I don't care about your past"
Was the immediate answer he received.
Yet he questioned if he was worthy.
He found it hard to believe.

"How can you love me?"
"How could you take me back?"
"My soul is lost without hope
and my heart is cold and black."

The reply transformed his heart.
"I knit you in your mother's womb."
"I died for you upon that cross."
"I left behind only an empty tomb."

"I loved you deeply on that day
and I love you just as much now."
"I am the one who heals your pain."
"To me every knee will bow."

"I surrender to you my Lord!"
"I give you every part of me!"
"I am a captive to my pain
and I pray you set me free!"

Sorrow transformed to joy;
Shame transformed to grace.
It all started on that day
when he met his Savior face to face.


       The lies of this world run deep. They are the false foundation for the ways we will find joy, peace, acceptance and love. Yet they all have conditions. Those conditions are often led off by a simple, two letter word; "if." "If I only had _____ I would be worthy." "If I only did _____ I could find peace." "If I only were _____ then I could be loved."

Fill in your own blanks and draw new statements for that matter.

## Lost And Found

Standing on the corner of nowhere and forever;
he stares forlornly down both of the roads.
The burden of his sins weighing heavily upon him;
his greatest desire, to lighten this crushing load.

He is beaten, bloodied and bruised from his choices.
Never had he experienced this truth called grace.
The years of his wander lust had taken their toll;
they were etched into the lines on his face.

How had he arrived at such a desolate place?
For so many years he experienced nothing but "alone."
The pain of his self imposed isolation nagged.
Deep gashes lay open exposing tissue and bone.

It seemed to him that there was no one to cry out to.
There was no one who cared about his desperate plight.
He wished secretly for death to overcome him.
He hoped that it could bring a peace greater than this night.

Surrounded by an endless sea of humanity;
yet he wondered if anyone noticed he was there.
It's easy to come into proximity with people
but almost impossible to find someone who cares.

He knew that he wore his brokenness on the outside
and wondered if others were covering what was within.
It seemed to him that life was a constant battlefield.
He was fighting a war he could not win.

He wondered if anyone out there could hear him.
He wondered if anyone in this world cared.
Even the simplest human touch was denied of him.
It was if he was a leper and no one even dared.

He was expectant of a life of continued isolation
So he was shocked to feel someone touch him from inside.
It seemed that this touch came from the very center of him
and there was nothing left for him to hide.

The voice from within said, "I see you!"
He knew instantly that these words spoken were true.
Confusion began taking over his weary heart
and he was uncertain as to what he was to do.

"Call my name, my friend. You already know who I am."
Some of the people had to have seen him fall to his knees.
The heat on of the city was stifling that day.
But inside of him he felt a cool and refreshing breeze.

If he had only known that forgiveness was available for the ask-
ing
Perhaps he wouldn't have run so far and for so long.
This voice continued welling up from within him
singing a sweet and melodic song.

His heart finally felt "home" within this breeze
as he heard the words that were softly spoken.
"Bring your wounded and afflicted.
I will make whole that which was broken."

He never knew just how much he needed a Savior
until he discovered just how far he could fall.
But it was in this place he cried out to Jesus
finding that he was there to answer his desperate call.


Some of us hide our brokenness in dark corners of our souls while others wear it out on our sleeves. Jesus came to heal us; to set us free of this bondage of sin. He came to make what was broken whole. Are you feeling the weight of your pain this morning? He sacrificed it all to reach you, to heal you, to love you, and to spend forever with you. Will you accept his gift?

## Lover of My Soul

Just calling out your name
brought tears to my eyes.
When I asked you to come
I know you heard my cries.

You entered in with me
as I confessed my fear of falling.
Stepping forward was not without risk
but I could not ignore your calling.

I now bear my heart before all
so You may be honored and praised.
I will not relinquish this mission
until I reach the end of my days.

When I suffer and I mourn
I will remember the price to be free.
It was you who suffered for all mankind.
It was you who died upon that tree.

Your love for me is undeniable
You have proven it again and again.
You loved me before I even knew you.
You paid a high price for my sin.

How can I not sing your praises
before the whole of the earth?
I was a dead man walking
You showed me life through new birth.

I gladly give up my old selfish ways.
Their joys were short lived at best.
I am distanced as far from them
as the east is from the west.

You removed these moth ridden clothes
and along with them many chains.
No longer am I alone in my suffering.
You enter into even my deepest pains.

Your love is deep and it is wide.
You are able to cure the greatest pain.
Your grace and mercy endure forever
and it is forever that you will reign!

Friends, you may wonder what it means
to enter into a journey of grace.
It means you can stop running from Him.
Stop and accept his warm embrace.

So my friend, do you know the healer?
Do you know the one who sets captives free?
If you are bound in chains on this day
He is the one who holds the key!


It is my honor and privilege to share many aspects of my life and my walk with the Lord. I have dark past. I have a long list of things to be ashamed of. I found my freedom through a real and personal relationship with Christ Jesus and although I am walking out with scars from many years of bondage, I am free.

When I first started this group, I had a single desire that was laid upon my heart. I wanted to reach out to the many broken people who, like me, have longed for freedom but never dared to dream of it. I am here to tell you that it's yours for the taking. He doesn't judge you and neither do I. So come out of the shadows. Come out of the dark alleys. Come out, come out, wherever you are!

## Majestic

You stand beside me
on this most glorious day.
You have captured my heart
and you will never go away!

Oh great lover of my soul
how magnificent is your grace!
I see only eyes of understanding
as I look upon your face!

You do not hide yourself from me.
With you I know I will want not.
You stand with me in the battle.
With you, victory in each that is fought!

You have heard the cries of your people
and you have set the captives free!
They stand whole before us all
so that believers are made of all who see!

Oh my Master!
My most glorious King!
You fill my soul with your living waters
And I want for nothing!

Your Spirit fills me
with a peace surpassing my wildest dreams!
I pray that I may stay in this place
where only to you will I cling.

I shout your praises
from the highest mountain top!
I shout of your magnificence
and nothing can make me stop!

Your pure white snow has fallen
and has covered my imperfections
Only this white covering can be seen
from any direction!

So I praise you in this song.
I celebrate you in these words.
May we boldly approach your throne
and know that we will be heard!


So much of the religious system seems to be built around the notion of "pleasing God." We work and strive reaching out and hoping that what we have done will be an acceptable offering to Him. We adopt terms like "sin management" to achieve a status of worthiness before Him. Yet I don't believe that He is pleased with these offerings. In reality there is NOTHING that we can do that will make us worthy. However, for those of us who accept the gift Christ gave us in dying on the cross, we are ALREADY worthy! He never said I love you IF. He said I love you (period).

When I wrote this poem I was rejoicing. The night before had been long and I was up late. But this morning I was filled with the reminders of God's grace. I know that many struggle with the whole concept. I was one of them. I strived with all that was within me to EARN grace and yet it had already been given to me. The price for the giver was high but the cost for me is NOTHING. The same is true for YOU. Are you ready to lay down all of your self righteousness and trade it for HIS grace? I assure you, He is eager to give it to you!

## My Prison Wall

Maybe I wasn't designed
to reside in this world of pain.
Reaching out for the love of others
burned me time and time again.

So I made up plans
on how I could withdraw.
I obtained all the brick and mortar
to begin building this wall.

The bricks were placed in slowly;
carefully laid one at a time.
My budget for construction was small
but I gladly spent every single dime.

The day came when this wall was complete
and behind this barrier did I reside.
It kept me safe from this world.
It gave me a place where I could hide.

Yet in all of this careful construction
I had neglected to build a door.
My solace became my isolation
as no one could reach me anymore.

Sometimes I longed for human touch
and to feel another's warm embrace.
This wall had imprisoned me.
There was no escape from this place.

Years of food stores were running low
and the well was running dry.
I had just enough each day
to barely get by.

One morning at the days early dawn
I scaled my wall to feel the warmth of light.
I had slept alone in my tomb as always
and a chill had pierced me in the night.

On the horizon a figure headed my direction.
I had to shield my eyes before his shape became clear.
He was headed deliberately towards me.
It was obvious that he was headed here.

He carried a sledgehammer
It was held high so that I could see.
If he knew the nature my predicament
surely he would know I could not be free.

He took his first swing
The sound of steel meeting hardened clay.
He didn't slow down there
as he continued to break bits of wall away.

He was slightly built.
Yet it was obvious that he was quite strong.
Between each blow of the hammer;
he didn't hesitate long.

When he did rest for just a moment
I saw on the hammer's handle was written "LOVE."
I recognized his face now
and knew he came from above.

He made short work of my wall.
I anxiously climbed down to see.
There was now a large hole in the brick
and I was finally set free.

As I walked outside for the first time in years
my first touch was his warm embrace.
His eyes told me that he already knew me
when I gazed upon his face.

He told me wherever I traveled;
he would always be there.
I could leave this wall behind me
and experience love from anywhere.

I carried with me my liberator's hammer
as I set out once again into this land.
He taught me how to break down other's walls
using only the might of HIS hand.

So I cry out to all
from the top of the highest hill.
You can come outside of your walls.
Your freedom is the Master's will!


I began constructing my wall when I was a child. When I felt ashamed I would add a brick. When I felt inadequate I would lay some more mortar. When I felt undesirable and unloved I would lay low behind whatever wall I had in place to protect me. Yet as I constructed my wall over the years I forgot a basic principle. Walls are constructed to create separation. My wall was effective at keeping the people and the pain out, but it was also effective at trapping me within. The wounds I had received didn't heal. There was no one there to minister to them. Yet there was that nagging fear. Who would be there to protect me? Jesus answers this question clearly in John Chapter 10 verses 7-10 when he says, *"I am the Gate for the sheep. All those others are up to no good—sheep stealers, every one of them. But the sheep didn't listen to them. I am the Gate. Anyone who goes through me will be cared for—will freely go in and out, and find pasture. A thief is only there to steal and kill and destroy. I came so they can have real and eternal life, more and better life than they ever dreamed of."* He IS the gate that creates freedom from the wall. He is also the protector that keeps the thief at bay. His word is true and he can be trusted.

Are you living behind a wall? Does it still feel like it's protecting you or do you miss true love and companionship? Maybe you are looking for someone who can break down that wall so you can experience freedom. Cry out! Cry out now! Freedom can only come through love and I know the lover of your heart!

## My Reflection

You look at me intently.
I smile back at you.
My mask is in place firmly.
I hope you don't see through.

Like a game of poker
you see only what I show.
I hide the emotion and pain.
and hope that you won't know.

But when I look in the mirror
I can't hide what I see.
I can't help but see past the mask
down deep into the real me.

The ugliness within
bounces back from my reflection.
I am lost and wandering
hoping desperately to find direction.

I cannot cover my sins
no matter how many masks I wear.
Sometime they overwhelm me
beyond what I am able to bear.

Then the streaming of tears
like a dam that has burst.
I recollect a powerful story
about how Jesus loved me first.

He loved ME
and yet I am sick and depraved.
I sought all that was sinful
but forgiveness I always craved.

I remember the picture I saw
of him with his arms wide open.
I fall to my knees before him
broken but desperately hoping.

Oh Jesus!
Are your arms still open to me?
If I lay my life down before you
will you still set me free?

Will you forgive this life of sin?
Will you show me your grace?
I feel your arms stretched wide
and know I can show my true face.

On my knees I was broken
now back on my feet I am whole.
My cup was empty and dry
but now it is exceedingly full.

I FEEL your love!
It courses through my veins.
How could I not share your forgiveness?
And how I will never be the same!


    This morning I read a powerful story of transformation. The truth is, every story of transformation is powerful but this one really touched me. We are in world filled with lost and broken people desperately trying to find their way. We are slaves to our sin and pain. We wear the shackles of our suffering, forever dragging us down. I was there! I know this place all too well! I am here to boldly tell you that you don't have to stay there. If your heart cries out begging for something more what will you seek? If you always do what you always did, you will always get what you always got! Think about it. There is more out there. There is true freedom! The prison gates have flung wide open. I ran out of my cell. Nothing but freedom lies before me. Are there any other prisoners who want to join me on this jail break?

One of the greatest gifts that we have been given is the freedom of choice. You have the opportunity to make one today that will change your life forever!

## Nowhere to Run

Where darkness prevails
there can be no light.
Outside as bright as sun
inside, dark as night.

Windows to the soul
obscuring all inside.
A masquerade ball
energy spent to hide.

A heart so black
inside skin white.
Hidden like a coal
away from sight.

Whether the highest peak
Or the depths of the sea,
There is no hiding place
nowhere to flee.

So why toil?
Why slave away to sin?
There's no escape from destiny,
And in the end love will win!

Let Him take the darkness,
shine in his perfect light.
No longer a candle under a bushel
Now out in plain sight.

It matters not where you've been,
Only what lies ahead.
He walks beside you now,
showing the path to tread.

So surrender,
and find true victory.
The chains are broken
so that you can be free!

## On the Edge

Locked up tight.
She's been here before.
Shutting the world out
on the other side of the door.

Now finally safe
the drops begin to fall down.
If she let all the tears inside out
she would surely drown.

Memories of her childhood
force their way into her head.
The anguish of her suffering
makes her wish she were dead.

Slowly with hesitation
she reaches for the drawer.
Knowing what she needs;
she's been here before.

Now she has it in her hand;
this small but sharp blade
If she could cut the memories out
surely she could make them fade.

Now that it's close to her arm
she begins to battle with her nerve.
She can see the headlights coming
and she is tempted to swerve.

There is no escape from this pain.
Her mind is filled with doubt.
She begins to wonder about true love
and wish she knew what it's about.

One choice never ending suffering;
the other brings an uncertain death.
Maybe she could find some peace
before she breathes her last breath.

Then a new voice in her head
saying "fear not, I am here."
She's heard this voice before
but its been so many years.

She had tried this "Jesus guy" before
but he didn't seem to protect her then.
How could she possibly find the faith
to put her trust in him again?

"Oh Lord please help me!"
"I am so very afraid!"
"I can't take the hurting anymore
but I don't want to end it with this blade!"

"If I trusted you now
would you restore my heart?"
"Could you make me whole again?"
"Could you give me a fresh start?"

Then a response almost audible
as if he were standing right there.
"I have never been far from you
and yes, I do still care!"

The blade falls to the floor;
as does she.
REAL hope fills her heart
as she prays on bended knee.

"Oh Jesus, can you still love me?"
"Can you take me just as I am?"
The tears begin pouring again
like water breaking through a dam.

A new sense begins to come to her.
It's the sense of peace.
She cast her sorrows freely on Jesus
and was finally released!


Have you ever felt trapped with no way out? Maybe you are there today. The pain of the past can strangle out all hope of real, lasting peace. You find yourself with shame holding you fast like an anchor holds a boat. Waves come in this life but when you are at anchor, its difficult to roll with them. There is no freedom! Oh what it would be like to release that weight and sail far, far away from it!

Have you heard his voice? He's calling out your name! He took on all of your shame so you wouldn't have to. He's stands by ready to cut away the anchor. It takes a leap of faith to believe the voice of truth, but its well worth taking!

## You Cared Enough

When I was in dark and desperate places,
You cared enough to show me your face.
When I was drowning in my sin,
You cared enough to show me grace.

When I was running as hard as I could,
You cared enough to chase me.
When I was wrapped and bound by chains,
You cared enough to set me free.

When I was lost and blinded by my wicked desires,
You cared enough to open the eyes of my heart.
When I was enveloped by gloom and darkness,
You cared enough to give me a fresh start.

When I was so full of holes and was sinking,
You cared enough to make me whole.
When I was lost and emptied of all purpose,
You cared enough to make me full.

When I was crying inside and hidden in shadow,
You cared enough to pull me out into the light.
When I was too weak to carry on with this journey,
You cared enough to teach me how to fight.

When I was a broken vessel holding nothing,
You cared enough to pick up all of the shards.
When I was hard and calloused on the inside,
You cared enough to soften a heart so hard.

When I was too weak to continue on this road,
You cared enough to wrap me in your arms.
When I was self destructive and dangerous,
You cared enough to save me from harm.

When I was too ashamed to hold my head up,
You cared enough to heal my deepest sorrow.
When I was weeping bitter tears of hopelessness,
You cared enough to show me hope for tomorrow.


Much of my life was spent running. I ran from the hopelessness inside of me. I ran from the thoughts of what tomorrow would bring. I ran from a purposeless existence. I ran from the hurt of days passed. Yet, with all of the running I did, I couldn't escape reality. None of the tools that I had at my disposal could help me evade the truth. Rather than healing me, my self help techniques brought me to deeper pits of despair. I needed a Savior! I was never going to be good enough. I was never going to be strong enough. I was never going to have enough willpower. I cursed God for my weakness. I determined that there was something fundamentally wrong with me yet I continued to strive under my own power. Jesus said, I am the way, the truth and the life. I knew this and yet I saw it as more of an expression than a reality. What words could I use to convey my gratitude to him for not giving up on me?

Where is your heart? Do you still have hope in self help? How is it working for you?

## Outside the Gate

I could not loose the chains
that kept me bound.
Many times I tried in futility
but no freedom could be found.

I propped my weakened soul up
against the wall of my prison.
So many solutions I had attempted;
now I was filled with indecision.

Clearly I was unable to break
through chains made of steel.
Chafing wounds left their mark
and they would not heal.

Guards stand outside my cell.
They taunt me with their lies.
One thing they said I believed;
surely here is where I would die.

I secretly wished for the end;
hoped that it would come quickly.
The years of captivity took their toll
as I became more sickly.

Another lonely night approached.
The sheer blackness crept in.
Again there were dreams of freedom;
again hopes of escape from this sin.

I pushed the thoughts from my mind
as it seemed best not to hope.
So often accepting my imprisonment
seemed the best way to cope.

In the pure blackness of midnight
came suddenly a marvelous light.
I had to shield my eyes from it
as it literally pierced the night.

I cowered in my corner;
uncertain as to what to expect.
Never before had my eyes beheld
a light that was so perfect.

The light source stood before me now
as I mustered my nerve to look upon his face.
His smile was unmistakable
and his eyes spoke of true grace.

As he reached out his hand
my eyes began to fill with tears.
I reached out only as a response
able to finally overcome my fears.

My chains gave way
and fell immediately to the ground.
No longer did they bind me
as my freedom had been found!

Now I held his hand tightly
as the prison gate opened wide.
After only a few short steps
we were on the outside.

I peered back into my cell
I knew this look would be my last.
Hope and joy now filled my heart.
My captivity was in the past.

There is something about the imagery of imprisonment and darkness that continues to draw me back in. When I search for metaphors of what my life felt like before Christ Jesus interceded on my behalf, there is no better image to describe it than this. I was born into captivity. Even the supposed innocence of childhood was overshadowed with these issues that were innate to me. I put on my first masks when I was quite young. They became the first signs of my imprisonment. Once I put on my first mask and began the world of make believe, it seemed impossible to take it off. To take off the mask meant ending the façade. It meant confessing my true identity. Not only was I afraid of being subject to that scrutiny, I was afraid of being proven a liar by projecting such a false front. Still, my greatest fear was that the real me was not worthy to receive real, unconditional love. When compared with the utter rejection I anticipated if I were to let my true self show through, the mask felt like protection. Still, I was a prisoner. I constructed the walls then placed the bars myself. At first I believed the prison to be a refuge. It wasn't until years later that it's true nature was revealed. My refuge had become isolation and my prison had become inescapable.

Many out here reading this morning know this prison. Maybe you never quite thought of it in these terms but when we choose to place these masks on our faces we begin to deny the brokenness that resides within us and replace it with a false front. Yet there is one who can remove the masks and fix the broken places beneath them. His name is Christ Jesus. For me this is not a theory or a belief. It is a reality! I speak from my own personal experience! So, if your mask has morphed from the costume you wear to the masquerade ball into something more like the iron mask which is secured by lock and key, you have a choice. Hold on to pretend and hope you can endure or give yourself over to the one who can set you free. Like with me, the choice is yours.

## Prayer For Deliverance

From my feet
I fall to my knees.
I cry out your name now.
I pray you hear my pleas.

Oh Lord
my world is falling apart.
If this is not my end
I pray for a fresh start.

This heart you have created
is slowly becoming a tomb.
Water is coming in the cracks
of my little room.

Oh Lord
In my sorrow I may drown!
My castle is made of sand
the walls are crashing down.

Free my heart from these thorns.
Free my mind from these chains.
Take all this pain away from me
until only you remain.

Transform my desires
and model them after yours
Teach me your ways
until only love endures.

Take this broken vessel,
put it in its perfect place.
Until the day I leave this earth
to meet you face to face.

Be my perfect master.
Be the king on my throne.
Turn skepticism to trust.
Don't ever leave me alone.

Oh Lord
be the God of this nation.
Be the lover of my heart.
I am in need of transformation!

Take my hand today Lord
and put me to your use.
Embrace me in your loving arms.
Never turn me loose.

I pray this in the name of my Savior;
in the name of Jesus
The very one who gave his life.
The one who holds the key to free us!

I recently posed a question on my Facebook account. It read, "Mitch Salmon is wondering if you will answer this question... The doctor tells you that you have 1 day to live. Tomorrow before sun up you will die. What will you do with your last day on earth?" I received an abundance of answers to this question. Apparently this is a hot topic. One answer in particular struck me. The young lady said, "It doesn't really matter, because you can't change in one day." I engaged her in private dialog and in my last message I said, "I believe that everyone has that opportunity for one day to be a turning point. After all, a whole life can come down to one decision. It doesn't have to be on the last day of your life. It can be on any day, but usually its that one where you have sunk to the lowest depths. I know this to be true, because I experienced that one day myself and have never been the same since." Have you experienced that day? When you hit bottom, who did you cry out to? Maybe today is that day for you. He knows your pain. He longs to free you! Will you trust him, or continue to try and endure?

## Prayer for Rain

I look at the earth below,
Just rock and soil.
Yet it produces life
Through man's toil.

I look at the sky above,
laden clouds and blue.
Yet when the rain falls
It produces every color and hue.

I sense your spirit inside me
It makes me who I am.
It bursts out uncontained
like water from a broken dam.

I see your gifts around me,
also the broken and ashamed.
I pray for your healing in them
that they will never be the same.

For when the thirsty crave,
There is living water for their need.
For what the starved desire
There is food for those who take heed.

We need you to fall on us
like the ground needs the rain.
Only your cleansing power
can wash away the pain.

I implore you, do not leave us dusty
Do not leave us dry.
Shadow your clouds above us
And bring your rain from the sky.

We are your wild flowers.
We are your lilies of white.
Yet we need your food from heaven
to burst through the earth into sight.

Much of my life I was spent as a dead man walking. I trudged through one day and into the next. It hurt to even consider meaning and purpose. There simply was none that I could find. It was at the point of greatest anguish that God brought down his rain into my life. Wind no longer blew the dust of my dry soul. Where there had only been rocks and soil there were now flowers in bloom!

Does your life feel dry and dusty? Do you lack life and purpose? Maybe it's time to pray for rain!

## *Savior of Mankind*

Why do we shy away?
Why do we deny?
How can we question
all the stars in the sky?

We were created for a purpose.
We were created to be with you.
Yet among the many
You have chosen only the few.

Who are we
to be called by your name?
Are we the reason
that you came?

You died for us all.
You hung on that tree.
You sacrificed yourself
so that men could be free.

You could have turned your back.
You could have denied us that day.
You could have called the angels
to simply whisk you away.

But you stood your ground.
You made a stand for love.
You stayed true to your mission.
You were sanctified from above.

The son of God
became the savior of man.
No one truly understood
that it was his master plan.

The God who became human,
The sacrifice for us all.
It was you my sweet Jesus
who took the ultimate fall.

I should have died on that day.
I should have hung on that cross.
I should have been the one
to have experienced this loss.

So I bow before you now
and I honor your name.
For I know that without you
life could never be the same.

We are free!


How can those of us who are Christians walk around with
an air about us? Who are we anyway? We are redeemed sinners,
nothing more, nothing less! We were bought with a price and that
price was Christ's blood on a day that will live in history but
creates a future for us all. If you have accepted this gift, who have
you told about it? If you haven't, why would you reject something
that was so freely forgiven? Forget the church that judges. Forget
the people who hide behind self righteousness. Focus on the price
that was paid for you. Focus on the perfect love given to a fallen
people. This is the gospel. This is the good news! Do you have a
hole inside of you? Do you long to be whole instead? This is more
than a matter of eternity. It is a matter of right here, right now! This
is a call for all those who are slaves to sin to drop their chains. This
is a call for the broken to become to be restored! What are you
waiting for? Don't let me get in your way!

## Sensing the Creation

When I look upon the stars in the sky
I can't help but call out your name.
A million points of light shining before me;
each evidence of your glorious fame.

When I smell the fragrance of a flower
the sweet aroma permeating the air.
I am drawn to you like the bee to honey,
laying down my heavy burdens in your care.

When I look at the waves of green grass
as they waive before me in the breeze.
I am amazed at the majestic brilliance
that was endowed upon us with such ease.

When I see the sun ablaze at noon;
a magnificent ball of shining light.
I ponder the delicate nature of our existence;
understanding every day comes with a night.

When I feel the freshness of a gentle breeze
as it lightly brushes by my face.
I am reminded of how you surround me
wrapping me in your warm embrace.

When I touch the ruddy, damp soil,
feeling the moist grainy texture in my hand.
I see new life springing up from it,
renewing the resources of our land.

When I hear the roar of the ocean
it's almost as if your voice is in the din.
Each wave crashes on the shore before me,
returning to the sea your love pulls me in.

Everything I taste, touch, smell, hear and see
is a reminder of the undeserved grace I receive.
All of these wonderful creations of your hand,
remind me of the abundance of reasons to believe.


When I truly open my eyes to view the world around me I am amazed by God's creativity. Think about it… The creation that surrounds us is so vast and diverse. We experience colors and hues that stretch beyond our own imagination! We see, feel, touch, taste and smell so many different things that we take for granted. When was the last time you gave pause to give thanks to our Creator for the abundance marvels in your life?

## Standing Before Giants

I stand on the field of battle,
with only a sling and 5 small stones.
Yet I know my God is with me,
and because of faith I am not alone.

Fear demands that I run
but courage calls me to stand.
For this single battle of warriors
will decide the ownership of this land.

The mightiest warrior faces me,
and laughs when he sees my size.
But he knows not my God;
knows not how soon his demise.

He howls with laughter,
and lowers his guard.
With a single well placed stone
he hits the ground hard.

As with the bear and the lion,
I have defended my flock.
Now it is the warriors of Israel
who stand their ground and mock.

The fallen Philistine giant,
lies helpless before my feet.
I draw a sword I can barely manage,
steel and flesh finally meet.

Now at the end of the day,
the Lord's shepherd boy sees victory.
The mighty warrior has fallen
and lies dead for all to see.

Faith defeats might.
His word pierces the shield.
The proud are humbled.
With bended knee all will yield.


Most know the story of David and Goliath. We know that a very average sized boy (David was still in his teens) faced off against a 9 foot giant. I have a tendency to take for granted the amount of faith and courage this took. Yet as I read the story (found in 1 Samuel 17:1-51) I can see that David expressed no fear. He stood before the giant in a fight he was sure to lose, if evaluated by the world's standards. The odds in Las Vegas would have been 1,000 to 1 yet David knew something that no one else understood. He knew WHO was on his side!

We may not face physical giants in our lives but we certainly face emotional and spiritual giants. As we stand before them we know that they could conquer us with one crushing blow. Addictions tear at us. Relationships that are on the rocks drive us down. Selfishness isolates us. Tragedies cause us to question our faith. These are just a few of the things that we face. Fill in the blank with your own. Now ask yourself, "Who is in my corner?" Do you know the one who conquers giants? Don't be conquered. Don't be destroyed. Call out his name now and he will join you in the fight!

## Surrendering All of Me

A surrender of self
to one who is much greater than me.
I may be peering through dense fog
but He can always see.

He beckons me forward
with a strong yet gentle outstretched hand.
He places my home upon the rock
far removed from the shifting sand.

He calls me by name.
He describes me in ways before unheard.
He opened the door of my cage
and set me free like a bird.

He provides my soul with the necessities
then keeps filling until I overflow.
He protects my heart from danger
and remains with me wherever I go.

Master, Redeemer, and Friend.
All of these things He has become to me.
Never does He ignore my cries.
He always answers my most urgent pleas.

So on bended knee
I seek with urgency the will of the King.
He remains constantly on His throne.
He welcomes the needs that I bring.

Surrender? What have I surrendered?
A selfish and dead existence never knowing more?
He called me to know new adventures
as He prepares me for what's still in store.

Do you have a fear of losing control? Believe me, I can relate. Most of my life was spent with me at the driver's wheel. The signs were there telling me I wasn't a competent driver but I ignored them all. I was so afraid of losing control of my life and missing out on something. I chased every promise that I could dream of in this world. Many of them I obtained. Yet I still felt empty and lost. To find my true self, I had to know my identity in God. I was created by Him for Him to love Him. Only when I acknowledged and accepted this did I find the peace and joy that would fill that huge hole within me. So what did I give up? I gave up a life of chasing shadows. I gave up a life of spitting into the wind. To these things I say, "Good riddance!"

So, what are you holding onto? What dreams do you continue to chase? Are you starting to get the idea that there is no true fulfillment in them? Listen to me. Until you let go you will never understand the fullness of God's love and the peace that only He provides.

## The Crossroads

When facing the crossroads,
We have a choice on the path to take.
Our very destiny depends
On the decisions we make.

One road is narrow,
And yet the path is barely worn.
When we face the cross roads of intention
We are often torn.

The other road is wide,
and seems easy to travel.
It is grated smooth,
And covered with gravel.

Crossing from one to the other
Is not easy but it can be done.
It may seem perilous,
But it leads to the Son.

So each must choose,
Each must answer for their choice.
So cry out now
So that He will hear your voice.

Now stay the course
And he will guide your way.
He will walk beside you
Each and every day.

If you stumble,
He will catch you in his arms.
He will protect you
From any real harm.

Enter the narrow gate
Into your promised home.
The path was not easy,
But you were not alone!

## The Dance

Even when I was young
the sickness was there.
Since that time
it has followed me everywhere.

The chains that bind
reside inside of me.
I could never break them
yet I longed to be free.

I fell and shattered
until I was truly broken.
I portrayed my nature
with every word that was spoken.

I ran and I hid
when there was nowhere to hide.
No matter how far I traveled
I couldn't escape what was inside.

So I cried out your name
in the most pitiful of ways.
I waited for you while running
through all of my days.

I am an enigma;
a walking contradiction.
Seeking who I truly am
through all of this affliction.

Running and yet standing;
hiding in plain sight.
Out in the light of the sun
and yet longing for night.

Oh, that the darkness could cover
all of my guilt and shame!
Oh, that someone could come
and call my true name.

I hear the word righteous
and know that it could not be me.
Some say that I am loved
yet I wish that I could see.

So I continue to run in my place.
I continue to make my desperate stand.
I continue to step forward
in this dry and desolate land.

I decide to trust in you
despite all that I am feeling.
I rely on your miracles
to bring about my healing.

Will you be that cord in my life
which is not easily broken?
If I pray to you now
will you hear the words that are spoken?

I believe you are here
and yet at times you seem far away.
I believe I am rooted in you
and yet I panic when I sway.

So hold me now
and never let me go.
I need you more each day;
even more than you know.

Last night, when I wrote this I could feel every word. The reality of my feelings boxed me in and I put on the blinders. The funny thing about feelings is that they are so hard to see beyond. Our feelings become our realities. Yet they shift and sway. They betray us in lies. These realities are untrue and yet they FEEL like the kind of wall that cannot be scaled, dug under or traveled around. Yet these walls exist only in our minds. I'm not here to tell you how you can overcome these things. I struggle with them myself. I am here to point out the things that I have learned. The truth can sometimes feel like a lie and a lie can sometimes feel like the truth. If that is the case, then our feelings cannot always be trusted. They will ultimately betray us if our decision-making is based on them.

How are you feeling? Are you feeling downtrodden? Do you feel like your life will never change? Do you feel unlovable? Maybe you FEEL like God is far away from you and that he doesn't care. Maybe you feel like you have it all together. That's just as dangerous as all of the other feelings. So what will you trust; the shifting sands of the latest feeling or the truth that remains constant regardless of how you feel about it?

## The Darkest Night

Out in the wide open spaces
as the first signs of dusk set in.
Red hues fill the lingering sunset.
Day is ending, soon night begins.

I make a fire for the night.
It will prove my closest companion.
As light and warmth permeate
there is still loneliness in this canyon.

Huddling in close to the fire now
Flickering shadows at the light's end
Beyond the glow of this small blaze;
a darkness against which I cannot defend.

These shadows dance just out of reach
like ancient savages preparing for war.
Blood lust fills their hearts
as they seek to settle the score.

The perceived safety of this light
slowly begins to fade away.
The mystery and terror of darkness
will not be held at bay.

With longing, I look to the night sky
but alas there is no moon.
Without adequate fuel for this fire
darkness will overcome me soon.

My preparation for this night was poor
I had not gathered adequate wood.
The insidious darkness grows ever closer
threatening to destroy all that is good.

Now the fire grows increasingly dim;
the panic setting in quickens my heart.
I hear snickering and howls in the darkness
as the unknown threatens to tear me apart.

Instincts of fight or flight
course through my terrified mind.
Yet there is nowhere to run, no way to fight.
These forces are hidden and I am blind.

Evil cackles fill the night
accusations form a formidable attack.
I have no excuses for my sinful ways
and no way to take them back.

The accusers know my weaknesses.
They use them to demand my surrender.
There is no grace according to them.
I stand guilty with no defender.

The tears well up from deep within
My end seems to be drawing near.
They attack with truth that knows no love
and I cower before them in fear.

Suddenly the powerful force of angelic wings
A loud says "My grace is sufficient for you!"
"My power is made perfect in your weakness."
Joy fills me for I know that this is true!

The shrieks now emanate from the tormentors.
They cannot stand in the presence of perfect love.
Their lies are drowned out by His mercy and grace
which pours down freely from above.

The dwindling fire that was my safeguard
Suddenly springs to life like a fiery furnace.
Now its brightness pierces right through the dark
and the demons flee in earnest.

I am still there but no longer alone
As I bask in the warmth of His true grace.
I avert my eyes from the brilliant glow
but find myself overjoyed as I see His face.


Shame has to be one of the most painful emotions we can experience. Coupled with its close cousin, guilt, they hobbled me for years. Each time I began to believe in and apply grace in my life; shame crept up to remind me of my past actions and my undeniable guilt. The enemy loves to point out to me all of my shortcomings and there are many! The truth is that I may not be worthy to talk about the good news. Perhaps that is more suited for someone who has always made the right choices. But then I have to wonder, who knows more about grace, the saint or the sinner? Jesus said plainly that he "came for the sin sick, not the spiritually fit." I certainly know what it means to be sick with sin! Paul says in Romans 5, *"But sin didn't, and doesn't, have a chance in competition with the aggressive forgiveness we call grace. When it's sin versus grace, grace wins hands down."* Wow! Now that is good news!

Are you living in shame? Does the enemy point his finger at you, saying, "Guilty?" I am here to tell you the good news of grace. Sin doesn't stand a chance against it! So with this abounding grace available to all who call Christ their master, maybe its time to stop focusing on our shortcomings. Maybe it's time to begin focusing on His face! He doesn't seek to condemn. He seeks to redeem us with His perfect love. Whether you know Him right now or not, you can call on His name. Maybe it's time you got to know one another!

## *The Darkness*

The thief of souls
comes to steal in the night.
So build a fire in my heart
and make it bright.

He stays among the shadows
seeking to devour.
Without your light
I'm weak and cower.

I must keep constant vigil
to keep the shadows at bay.
Staying strong as I await
the light of a new day.

Search my heart of Lord!
Reveal the weakness inside
So that I might stand strong
with nothing to hide.

Guard my heart closely
with your eternal word.
May it run deeply
now that I have heard.

Do not forsake me now
in this my darkest hour!
Do not give
The accuser power!

I will face the east
And seek the first light of day.
With eyes towards the sky
I continue to pray.

I cry out Oh Father!
The lover of my soul
Go to work in me now
and make me whole!

Oh Lord the night is darkest
just before the dawn.
Add the wood of your word
so my fire will remain strong.

Then my eyes behold
the first of the sun's rays.
And am finally assured
that all will be okay.

The darkness fades
as the light overpowers
Now it is the enemy
Who hides and cowers!

I stand tall
With hands raised high
Praising you now
As sun fills the sky.


1 Peter 5:8 *Be self-controlled and alert. Your enemy the devil prowls around like a roaring lion looking for someone to devour.*

Proverbs 4:23 *Above all else, guard your heart, for it is the wellspring of life.*

Deuteronomy 31:8 *The LORD himself goes before you and will be with you; he will never leave you nor forsake you. Do not be afraid; do not be discouraged.*

Darkness will come into our lives. We are assured that in this world there will be trouble. Still the darkness can only prevail for so long. We know that the light will return. Which way do you face? Are you looking to the east? Do you seek the light of a new day?

## The Fine Line

All of my life,
hidden in shame.
Pain piercing me like knives
with no one else to blame.

A heart that beats,
but a soul that is dead.
Fighting for freedom
from the demons in my head.

I hide away from you
I fear being found.
But I fear being lost
I hit the ground.

I cry out your name,
I pray for grace.
You bless my heart
and enter this place.

Now the fine line I walk
with the message of love.
No answers of my own
I point above.

For all who call you,
can find you where they are.
Although you may seem distant
you are never far.

Even in the depths of the sea
or in the skies above
there is nowhere to hide
from this message of love.

As he calls your name,
what will your answer be?
Are you content stumbling in the dark,
or do you long to see?

## The Hearts of Man

Pen is mightier
than the sword I carry.
So write these words
I will not tarry.

Men's hearts are hard.
They have become frigid.
Their wills cannot be bent.
Their souls are rigid.

Seeking earthly treasures
can take its toll.
What do they matter
when you lose your soul?

Oh Lord!
Hear my cries
It matters not what we possess
when the spirit dies.

I plead to you now
bring YOUR will to this land.
Make yourself known to us.
Show the works of your hand.

Your word is alive today
just as it was in days passed.
In the end your love
will be the only thing that lasts.

Do not leave us!
Do not forsake us in this time of need!
May the men who read these words
listen closely and take heed.

Do not store up your treasures
where the thief can steal.
Do not trade the spirit's longing
for what you can immediately feel.

Gratification is available immediately
but in the end it will not last.
Just like quicksand it sucks you in
and you are sinking fast!

What man would trade freedom
for the weight of chains?
Trade healing and wholeness
for hurt and pain?

Oh Lord!
Come into the hearts of men.
Show them the price you paid
to release them from their sin!


    In the American culture life is difficult. We may not face
the same immediate shortages of food and water that many other
countries face, but we do face corrupt morals. We are a materialistic
culture who tends to believe that by buying something we can
make our lives better. What fills the holes in your life? Are you
looking to something you can acquire? More importantly, where
are your greatest efforts spent? Do you invest your time and
energy into providing "stuff" or in giving of yourself? Our time
is precious because it's limited. All the money in the world
cannot buy us a single breath. There is no guarantee of tomorrow,
so if it all ends for you today what will be your legacy? I say
these things because I have fallen into this trap in the past.
I let ambition have precedence over the matters of my soul.
Don't follow in my footsteps through that land. The Lord can
show you a much better path! If today seems empty, even as you
are surrounded by your treasures, fill tomorrow with something
new. Fill it with the grace and love that our King provides!

## The Leper's Story

I am the leper.
I sit outside the city gate.
Passers sometimes take pity,
but mostly they hate.

I hear them talk,
I deserve this because of sin.
All doors are closed,
none will ever open.

I know not love,
only the pain of separation.
I am alone,
surrounded by an entire nation.

I felt no touch
for as long as I can recollect.
I must maintain distance from all
because of this defect.

I once heard of this man
they say his name is Jesus.
Many speak of him,
they say he will free us.

They say he makes the lame walk
He causes the blind to see.
If only I could find him
Maybe he would take mercy on me.

If only he came near,
I believe he could make me whole.
I could be free to touch.
My life could again be full..

Today I heard
that the master draws near.
My heart skips a beat
but I am overwhelmed with fear.

What if he were like the others?
What if he ordered me away?
I would be left to suffer,
in this progressive decay.

I set my fear aside,
to approach the king.
When the others notice me,
they back away and scream.

But he looks into my eyes,
and beckons me to draw near.
As I limp towards him
his eyes fill with tears.

I cry out
"If you are willing I can be clean!"
He laid his hands upon me
where all could be seen.

Many gasped and recoiled,
But my master remained
I could feel his healing touch
No longer viewed with distain.

Oh, I am whole
For the first time in years!
Freedom has replaced
All of these crippling fears!

I sing and dance,
I tell all who I see,
Go to my master Jesus,
So that you too will be free!

Mark 1:40 – 45

*A man with leprosy came to him and begged him on his knees, "If you are willing, you can make me clean."*

*Filled with compassion, Jesus reached out his hand and touched the man. "I am willing," he said. "Be clean!" Immediately the leprosy left him and he was cured.*

*Jesus sent him away at once with a strong warning: "See that you don't tell this to anyone. But go, show yourself to the priest and offer the sacrifices that Moses commanded for your cleansing, as a testimony to them." Instead he went out and began to talk freely, spreading the news. As a result, Jesus could no longer enter a town openly but stayed outside in lonely places. Yet the people still came to him from everywhere.*

Do you desire to be whole and free? When others turn their backs on you and keep you at arm's length there is one who won't. It is my master, Jesus. Do you know him? Have you felt his healing touch in your life? If you have not experienced healing, you can today! Fall to your knees and ask. He IS willing. He will not ignore your cries!

## The Mask

Whispers elevate to screaming
from the voices in my head.
Haunting me with lies;
telling me I would be better off dead.

The real pain of my heart
hidden behind a superficial smile.
Outside I appear "normal"
but inside I feel so vile.

A broken mirror
for my shattered soul.
Shards of glass scattered about
but a desire to be whole.

The deep pit of regret
filled to the brink with sorrow.
Naked and shameful;
afraid to face tomorrow.

Riddled with holes;
spewing out anger of the lost.
Damming them with anything
and no concern for the cost.

Wearing my mask
in the midst of this costume ball.
Can't release my grasp;
can't tear down this wall.

The enemy's arrows fly
and I with no place to hide.
A bloody battle rages
with no one by my side.

Homeless and penniless
wandering in search of feeling.
Shivering from the cold
dying desire for spiritual healing.

Desperately in need of a savior
willing to give anything for a friend.
Giving into hopelessness
waiting for my bitter end.

His love formed like a bridge
Solid ground under my feet.
His grace a cleansing rain
Finally hope to be complete.


   We wear masks to shield ourselves from the outside world.
I wore one for so many years that I started to wonder what I would
be like without it. See, with the mask I was able to project what I
thought the world wanted to see. If I was rejected, I still had a fall
back position. After all, I never revealed my TRUE self. Yet the
battle that raged inside was consuming me. To reveal this inner
turmoil, to take a risk of revealing lost faith, a chasm of hopeless-
ness, and a life of shame was more than I could handle. I found
myself isolated and alone. The mask hid me from the world, but
the resulting confusion of my facade made me feel unlovable. The
energy expended in "creating" my image made me feel inadequate.
Then there was the day that it all came crashing down. When I fell
to my face my mask was shed and I was exposed. I wept
as I repented. What was most overwhelming was my Father's
love. His words were clear, "I have forgiven you and you are good
enough." Are you tired of your own mask? Do you long for for-
giveness and to hear that you are good enough? Lay it down before
the King. His pardons are given freely. I am available to you if you
need someone to listen. Isn't it time you laid your burdens down
and traded them for freedom?

## The Pit

Opening my eyes
I begin to look around
but all around me is black
and I can't hear a sound.

I feel around below me
to find debris on the floor.
As I consider my circumstance
it's clear that I have been here before.

The darkness is all enveloping
like blindness in plain sight.
No one hears my cries for help.
No one joins me in this fight.

It is clear that I am alone here
and in complete desperation.
There is no chance of redemption;
no hope of salvation.

One thing is for certain
I must be free!
I claw at clay and mud
but fighting doesn't help me.

Shrinking into the darkness
I succumb to my shame.
I remember digging this hole now
and there is no one else to blame.

Surely I will die in this place
completely alone and afraid.
I'm suffering results of my actions
and my bed is made.

Then I begin to wonder
what if I called your name?
Would you answer my call again?
Would you free me from my shame?

Would you even hear my cries
from the depths of the abyss?
Even as I am separated from the world
it is you alone that I miss.

Oh my Savior!
Why do I bring myself to these places?
Oh my Lord!
Am I lost among all of the faces?

I don't deserve another chance.
I deserve to die here in this despair.
My suffering is justice.
My death would be fair.

I have to cover my eyes
as they are hit by a blinding light
The darkness is fully illuminated.
Glory has captured the night.

I look to the sky
to see a hand reaching from above.
Could this possibly be mercy?
Surely I am not deserving of this love!


We all come from some type of pit. Maybe we have fallen
into the same ones all of our life. Maybe we have so many that they
surround us. Regardless of our circumstances, we have a universal
language… it's pain. Sure we all have different perspectives on it.
Sure it's relative to our own tolerances. Still, the sad truth is that

we are a fallen people in a fallen world. Before we give up in utter despair, there is good news! Jesus loved us enough to come to this desolate place. He loved us enough to suffer and die on our behalf!

His love didn't end there. He loves us enough to extend grace to all who ask. He doesn't care where you have been. He doesn't care where you are right now. He will take you! He can pull you from the pit of your despair! Are you willing to believe it? As always, I am here if you need someone to talk to. I have been to some deep, dark places but I have been freed. The same freedom is available to all of us who are captives!

## The Price of Freedom

What was the price that was paid
for me to be free?
What else is there to the story of the three nails
piercing through flesh on that tree?

On this day humanity witnessed the death
of the only sinless man.
His selfless sacrifice
was the fulfillment of God's perfect plan.

He gave it all
and held nothing back
though he was brutalized
by his tormenter's attack.

He cried out our names.
He knew the ignorance of our deed.
So as he hung there dying
with his father he continued to plead.

He gasped for each breath
as his life slowly faded away.
He breathed new life into mankind
as he suffocated on that day.

What it must have been like
to look down on this world
in the few hours that changed forever;
on the day salvation's plan was unfurled.

Oh why my Lord
Would you die for a wretch like me?
Why did you pay such a high price
for me to be free?

I woke up in the middle of the night tonight. I couldn't sleep. When I finally got out of bed I made my way to the computer. Questions continued swirling in my head and as I brought them out to paper my questions became clear. What was the price paid for my freedom? The price paid was immense. I wasn't bought cheaply. How could he love someone like me that much? Paul sums what I am feeling up in Romans 5:8 when he says, *"We can understand someone dying for a person worth dying for, and we can understand how someone good and noble could inspire us to selfless sacrifice. But God put his love on the line for us by offering his Son in sacrificial death while we were of no use whatsoever to him."* So I am certainly not worthy of his sacrifice but I am grateful for it nonetheless. He didn't just die for me. He died for you as well. There is no act that you can perform which will set you right with God. The act was already performed. Forget all of the nifty religious slogans for a moment. Forget them forever if you like! The price that was paid for us boils down to seven hours on one Sunday. It boils down to the pain and suffering of one man for all of us. It boils down to a gift that was given to us. Have you accepted it?

The video I am sharing tonight is one I have never included before. It features scenes from the movie, "The Passion." This movie was rated R based on one thing alone. The depiction of Jesus' death is so violent that the film rating body had to restrict the audience. Jesus died an "R rated" death so that we could live a full life. He died so that we would know hope. If you do not know this hope that was brought to bear in his love, I invite you to now

## The Race

Stepping up to the start
my toe placed on the line.
The sound of a shot rings
and I leave it all behind.

I AM RUNNING

Exerting myself with my efforts
I finally find my stride.
Yet no amount of running
will separate me from what's inside.

I AM FALLING

Picking myself up
I feel the pain of broken knees.
I continue on wounded
but don't allow anyone to see.

I AM HIDING

Looking in all directions around
I see no other runners in the race.
I wonder to myself
why I keep this pace.

I AM WEARY

My heart is pounding in my chest
but I do not tell a soul.
Broken from my repeated falls
I wonder if I will ever be whole.

I AM SORROWFUL

Tears mingle with sweat
as I hold back the sobs.
A deep hurt resides within.
My peace and security it robs.

I AM DESPERATE

No one to hear my cries.
I am all alone in this place.
Even as I continue on
I can only see your face.

I AM LOST

The road I am on is foreign.
I fear that I have lost my way.
Fear and panic preside
but I hold them at bay.

I AM FOUND

In the distance ahead
hands waving high overhead.
Lost as I am inside
I am willing to be led.

I AM FREE

The hands that draw me in
are scarred from his sacrifice.
I am not deserving of freedom
But he says, "My grace will suffice!"

(For Moriah)

Life is filled with uncertainty but there is one thing that we can count on. We will experience pain along the journey. You don't need me to tell you this. Your heart already knows this fact. Whether your pain is upon you now or in the distant past, it is never forgotten. Some of this pain is the result of trauma we have endured at the hand of another. Some of it is from loss. Some of it is the result of our own actions. Each of us likely has experienced all of these categories. Regardless of the sources, there is one who came to heal them all and to offer us REAL life. His name is Jesus. He is the son of God. He died on a tree in the darkness. He was nailed to it by his own people. These were the very same people who lined the streets and cheered for him only a few days before. Trust me, he understands pain, whether it be physical, emotional or spiritual. He endured them all… willingly. So will you continue running lost on this road with wounded knees and a broken heart? Do you see him waving his arms ahead of you?

## The River of Sin

Standing on the bank of this river
with the current rushing by my feet.
I can travel no further on this path
and am ready to admit my defeat.

Questions course through my mind
as I consider what next to do.
I can't cross above these rapids.
I haven't the strength to swim through.

So I sit on this bank as I admit defeat.
My journey has certainly come to its end.
Then above the roar of the coursing water,
a whisper like a shout fills the wind.

"Trust me and I will show you the way!"
Whose voice was this calling out?
Was it real or did I imagine it?
My mind began to fill with doubt.

I looked back up to the distant shore
and saw the shape of this man.
His eyes spoke of a deep peace
as He motioned with outstretched hands.

But He was on the far shore
and I was trapped still on the near!
So desperately did I wish to reach Him
but my heart was still overcome with fear.

As I watched with eyes focused only on Him
I saw his right foot extend from the bank.
It clearly came into contact with the water
And yet it became firm and He never sank!

Then the left foot out onto the water
where the right foot had previously been.
Then one step continued following another
as He effortlessly crossed this river of my sin!

The rushing rapids were not too dangerous.
My pollution was not keeping Him away.
The tumultuous flow or my transgressions
were not enough to keep Him at bay.

Now half the river traveled
He stopped suddenly and again held out His hand.
Instinctively I knew what He desired of me.
My feet were also to leave the safety of dry land!

I hesitated for a moment as I was filled with doubt
but then considered the consequences of my distrust.
If He was willing to stand out in the river of my sin
Then joining him in the midst of it all was a must!

My feet stood atop of the waters
with no efforts that I can claim to be my own.
I joined Him there at the half way point
where He took my hand in His and led me home!


One of the common illustrations I hear for sin is that it is like this great chasm. We stand on one side of this bottomless pit and God stands on the other side. We have no way to cross and reach Him. Yet there is a bridge the reaches both sides and it is formed by Christ's sacrifice. For those of us reading this that don't know Jesus and haven't accepted his gift this is true. However, once we know him and choose to trust God, sin no longer forms a separation. He is willing to stand there right in the middle of it all! He is willing to stand beside us with his arm wrapped snugly around our shoulders as we examine these deep needs in our lives.

His grace is greater than any of our sins! It covers the sum total of them all! If you know him, why would you strive for righteousness? He has already declared you righteous! Why would you try to earn grace when it has already been given freely? If you don't know him yet, I want to tell you this. He already knows you and is a friend to you. He knows you and he wants a personal relationship with you! I'm not talking about a simple escape from condemnation (which is quite a feat in and of itself). I am talking about more abundant life that begins today and goes from there. Are you willing to leave this dry land that seems safe and yet imprisons you? Do you hear his voice? He beckons you. Will you answer and join him there?

## The Road Ahead

A voice whispers in my ear
I know that it is You, my King.
Calling me away from ordinary;
calling me to leave everything.

So I prepare my provisions
to take me who knows where.
One thing is certain;
wherever it is I am led
You will be there.

My pack is heavy
with the possessions I think I need
but you encourage me
to lighten my load.
You assure me of your faithfulness
YOU will provide
as I venture upon the open road.

I begin one foot before the other
with no idea where I am going.
My heart is uneasy
yet there is a certain freedom
in not knowing.

I watch many spectacular sunrises.
My small eyes are treated to a view
of enormous things.
The road unfolds one piece at a time
before me.
Each step uncertain of
what the next will bring.

You are my traveling companion
You are present with me each day.
You comfort me during the night
holding those
who would harm me at bay.

My every need is met
even before I utter the word.
Even my private thoughts
are before you.
As I say nothing
I know that I am heard.

Strange lands before me
yet you remind me that
wherever I may roam
when I lay my head down
I am always home.

No beast shall harm me.
You clamp their jaws closed.
Even they can sense anointing
Many an obstacle presents itself
You are faithful to steer me safely
through each hazard posed.

One morning before the dawn
You call me to my knees.
I kneel before you in worship
sensing your presence
in the warm, swirling breeze.

You speak to me
in words that I can understand.
"Child, I have brought you
safely thus far
but you are headed for
even more distant lands."

"One thing you can rely on,
wherever you are
I will be there too.
Even when you don't feel me
I will continue to see you through."

The wind died that moment
Your voice no longer
whispering to me.
I know not your plans
but I eagerly await to see.

So I continue on this journey
uncertain of what
is around the next turn.
I do not always see your face
or hear your words.
One of the many things unloaded
for this journey;
my worry and concern.


On Monday I shared with you a poem that was composed on Friday. I spoke of the real desperation I was facing as I struggled against doubt, loneliness and despair. The valley I had been standing in seemed to have 4 walls surrounding it and no means of escape. I reached out to many friends as well as the group during this time, sharing the pain I was experiencing. To be honest, I didn't anticipate an answer. While I was resolute to move on in faith, I didn't really expect anything from God. I was wrong. Yesterday morning I awoke at 4:30 and was wide awake. This isn't normal for me, at least as of late. I decided to get up and get ready for work. As I was going through my morning routine I was being bombarded with words of inspiration. When I got into the office I immediately began writing. The result is what you see above. They are more than mere words for me. They are a message from God.

Honestly, I didn't know what I had written until I finished and began to read back through what had come out. God was proving faithful in a deep time of need and His words are poured out in this poem.

Are you traveling the road this morning and wondering where God is? Perhaps you've grown weary and are now sitting on the wayside wondering when you will hear His voice again. Although you may not hear Him, it doesn't mean that He isn't there. Jesus tells us precisely where he is in this journey. In Matthew 28 he says to the disciples, *"God authorized and commanded me to commission you: Go out and train everyone you meet, far and near, in this way of life, marking them by baptism in the threefold name: Father, Son, and Holy Spirit. Then instruct them in the practice of all I have commanded you. I'll be with you as you do this, day after day after day, right up to the end of the age."* So, as we are called according to his purposes, he is with us always, even until the end of our time on this planet.

So this morning my friends, my dear brothers and sisters, I have the answer to my prayers. HE spoke these words just as much as I did. Hold tight folks and prepare yourself for the fact that His ways are not our ways and His thoughts are not our thoughts! You never know when you will turn and see Him there!

## The Sower and the Seed

The seed will be scattered
but not all ground will receive.
Many will be told the truth
and yet not all will believe.

Some will have the seed plucked away
before there is any chance to grow.
For them grace is as elusive
as the direction that the wind blows.

Some will receive the seed
but not allow it to sink in.
The new growth within will die
before it has a chance to begin.

Some will embrace the seed
and it will shoot up from the ground.
But the weeds of life will choke it out.
They will again become bound.

Yet some will find fertile ground.
Maybe it will only be a few.
These will embrace the seed.
They will seek what is true.

These will grow in abundance
to create a bumper crop.
They will produce seed of their own
so the growth will not stop.

The seed is the truth
and it is available to all.
We must receive with open arms.
We must answer the Master's call.

When we search it becomes evident
but only some are willing to see.
Only when we are open to the truth
will we be made free!


If you have spent much time reading the word, chances are that you have become familiar with the story of the sower and the seed. If you have never heard it before today, that's ok. You can find it in Luke 8:4-15. This story is simplistic yet it is only when we really ponder the elements of it that the meaning becomes clear. Based on the context, we are all ground. Some of us are hard. Some of us are surrounded by gravel, others are surrounded by the seeds of lies. Still there are some of us who are soft and ready to receive the seed. The seed, simply put, is the truth. It is the truth of grace. It is the truth of the father's love for us.

When I reflect on this story, I realize that at different points in my life I have been represented by each type of ground. At times in my life I have been so determined to do what "I" wanted to do that I was simply unwilling to acknowledge truth. At other times the seed has hit home but when faced with a truth based on faith versus the tangible world around me, I chose to pursue what I could see, feel and touch. I wanted the things of this world. I wanted the promises that it brought. I believed in the "American dream," thinking that it led to satisfaction and yet I was never satisfied. Then the day came when the seed fell on fertile ground. I was open to the truth only after I had believed so many lies and followed to them to their conclusion of emptiness, sorrow and shame. I was only open to the truth after I had eliminated every other possibility. I realize that not all people are like me. Some of you may receive this truth into fertile ground today. The truth, simply put, is this. God loves you. He loves you truly, madly and deeply. He desires to have a real and personal relationship with you. He sent his son, Jesus, to die for you. He paved the way so that you could have a personal relationship with him. He is willing and able to forgive all sin and transgression if you simply ask for it. It doesn't matter what you have done. He is willing to come into your heart if you simply ask him! The truth is so simple that we are willing to overlook it.

So which ground are you today? I imagine if you are the hard ground that the birds already swooped down and snatched this truth away from you. Maybe you are open to this truth but you are afraid of what will happen if you commit to it. Let me tell you, life will always have weeds but we don't have to let them choke us out. When we commit to believe the truth, God will give us the strength to grow far above them. The bottom line is that the truth is here within your grasp right now. Will you receive it?

## The Struggle Within

The answers were worth finding
but he had been searching for years.
He felt like there was so much to life
and he was grinding all of the gears.

Nothing came easily in this world.
It hadn't since he was a boy.
Somewhere along this journey
he had lost his sense of his joy.

Each new day he faced
presented new experiences in pain.
He smiled to hide the tears inside
but it was difficult to fain.

There was nowhere to run
and nowhere left to hide.
Where could he possibly go
to escape the emptiness inside?

The alarm clock went off
indicating the start of a new day.
Darkness pierced him even in the light.
It never seemed to go away.

His feet found their way to the floor
just as his heart sank in his chest.
A deep weariness penetrated him.
There was never enough rest.

What was this life for anyway?
Why on earth was he here?
The answers always eluded him
although sometimes they felt near.

He put a false smile on his face
while walking with a hurried stride.
He wouldn't show it to the world
but he was crying inside.

Suddenly chills pierced him to the core
like a flash of sudden light in the dark.
Morning dawned inside his heart
accompanied by the singing lark.

He knew the source of this awakening;
he dropped to his knees without hesitation.
The One who offered didn't need to ask twice.
He received this gift without reservation.

The fake smile melted like sun baked snow
and was replaced with authentic joy.
Years of jadedness were replaced.
Again he found that innocent boy.


Every step is an effort. Even the simplest gestures are cumbersome. I have been there... many times! The knee jerk response is to buck up, pull it together, and fix what's broken inside. Yet all of my self governed attempts, while they may have worked in the short term, have failed. My nights were haunted with dreams that I didn't understand and my days found me just trying to muster the energy to make it through. The next day, I simply repeated the process from the previous one. If you have been there, you know as I do, the weariness just compounds and the joy seems to slip further and further away. This world can do that to us. All the bluffing in the world cannot turn fiction into fact. It just turns us into actors. But what about the love and grace of God? When I go to these places of weariness and deep pain am I considering who HE says that I am? I would contend that what robs me of my joy is not circumstance so much as it is that I have lost vision of the truth.

What are your eyes focused on this morning? Do you have a real and personal relationship with the Lord? If not, I assure you that he wants to have one with you! If you do have a relationship with him, how are you defining yourself? Are you resting in the truth?

## The Way of Love

When I was called to love
I was far from His way.
Life was desolate and empty
living in a place I could not stay.

When I was called to love
my heart had become stone.
He molded it into something new
and would not leave me alone.

When I was called to love
I was stopped in my tracks,
Afraid of rejection and isolation
yet fear is something love lacks.

When I was called to love
I was a locked door.
He opened it wide with understanding
and the key to something more.

When I was called to love
I was forgiven of my sin.
He reminded me of the end story
and that love is sure to win.

When I was called to love
I was caught up in a rut.
My life was void of meaning
and to the quick I was cut.

When I was called to love
I was walking alone on the path.
Fearful of God's judgment
and sure of his impending wrath.

When I was called to love
He showed me that he knew my name
He set me on a new course
where life could never be the same.

When I was called to love
peace transcended my fret.
Long before my decision
He had paid my debt.

When I was called to love
I found new hope deep inside.
No longer was I separated from Him
Jesus had bridged the great divide!


      Have you been called to love? It is a tough decision that will require giving up what you want for what He wants. You will give up your plans for His. You will give up worry and trade it for faith. Jesus promises that his yoke is easy and his burden is light. In a day and age where men rarely honor their words, will you trust his? We are all given a choice. If your way isn't working, maybe it's time you give it up for his! When life's path narrows and only two will fit on the trail, who do you want by your side? People will fail you, but HE will not!

## The Wind and the Waves

Rowing across this sea of life
I begin to face the wind.
I continue pulling at the oars
Unaware trouble is around the bend.

The wind continues to increase
and the sea begins to churn.
Continuing under my own strength
with no reason for concern.

But as the swells continue to rise
no longer can I spot the shore.
Panic begins to grip my heart
slowly turning into horror.

Now the waves are looming
as they begin to crash over the boat.
The water is pouring in
and I wonder how I will remain afloat.

Continuing to struggle at the oars
I realize my efforts are in vain.
The once sunny skies of my journey
are filled with dark clouds and rain.

I am now in real trouble;
in full knowledge that I will drown.
I cannot survive these waters
when my small boat goes down.

With all my own powers futile
I fill my heart with fervent prayer.
I ask for mercy from these stormy seas;
that my lungs will continue to breathe air.

Then over the sound of the angry wind,
over the roar of the crashing seas.
I hear the words, "Quiet, settle down!"
Instantly I know he heard my pleas.

Who is this man commanding wind and waves?
Who reverses these skies of gray?
He took the stormiest night at sea
And brought back the light of day!

I have faced a number of storms in my life. It's amazing to me that even after experiencing so many self made disasters that I continue to try to rely on my own strength to bring me through. This is one lesson that I have learned with certainty… my control over situations I face is an absolute illusion. The more I believe these lies, the closer my boat comes to the rocks and certain death. I should have been a casualty to stormy seas many years ago, yet the grace and mercy of our Lord has seen me through time and time again.

Do you find yourself struggling at the oars even when it seems futile? When you feel the wind and sea in your face and you can't find the safety of shore, it's a sign that you are in trouble! Don't wait for your boat to be swamped. Let go of the oars and cry out his name. He is faithful to bring a story mercy in grace to a near tragedy at sea!

## Things Lost On the Journey

Walking down this road;
holding on to the hand of my Master.
I became weary and thus released.
My life became a disaster.

I rested and abided in you, my Lord
until I let the foundation give way.
Now I find myself searching for joy
unable to find it to this day.

Eternity with you,
is a promise with much allure.
Then somewhere I lost my hope
now I am no longer able to endure.

Living in your grace;
trusting you for each new day.
Then I began striving to earn
and let your perfect love slip away.

So I searched for these things
which I had somehow lost.
I searched every corner and cupboard
determined to pay any cost.

Yet my days remained gray
My heart filled with impending doom.
I tried to find a sincere smile;
but inside was nothing but gloom.

The cupboards were bare.
My streams had run dry.
I placed my head into my hands
and found the tears to cry.

I called upon your name,
But did not know where you were.
Without you I was so lonely.
My life was one big blur.

Then a vision overtook me.
It welled up from deep within.
It was a vision of a day of redemption;
the day that you took all my sin.

This is how my search ended.
I came upon a cross shaped tree
where my Savior suffered and died
so that I could be made free.

I saw you look down upon me
with arms that were pinned wide.
All of these mercies poured out
as the lance pierced your side.

I saw joy, peace, hope and love;
they rained down from the sky.
Like healing waters they fell.
My desert was no longer dry.


    This morning I woke up with the fruits of the Spirit occupying my mind. Thoughts swirled in my head literally from the time I opened my eyes. As I showered and got ready to go to work, the thoughts increased. Like pieces of a puzzle that were all jumbled, I knew that when they came together, the picture would become clear. Yet as I sit here with the keys of this keyboard under hand, I know the point at which I need to arrive, but no idea how to get there. See, when we put our faith in Christ Jesus and his sacrifice on our behalf we are no longer who we define ourselves to be. I am no longer just "Mitch." I am Christ in mitch. That old "Mitch" is gone! All of the shame, guilt and sorrow of my old ways are gone with the old me! So if you are reading this and wondering where I am headed, don't miss this. If you are searching for the fruits of the Spirit and are unable to find them, I want to tell you where they are. They are in Christ Jesus! I realize this may be vague if left here, so let me continue. As I said before, we are no longer defined by who we were. However, if we choose to hold onto that old definition we will find many of the same struggles as we did all along. We might even convince ourselves that nothing has changed within us. It's not until we trust His definition of us that we find our true selves. We are righteous and holy. We are saints! To be certain, this isn't because of who we are. It is because of who He is. So on my own, I am nothing. With Him I am the one that He defines me to be! This isn't based on an emotion. Emotions are fickle. They come and go. They mislead us much of the time. It is based on truth and truth NEVER changes.

I don't know where you stand personally this morning. Maybe you have experienced peace, joy, love and hope before but it is lost to you now. Maybe you have never trusted Him and continue to define yourself in the only ways that you know. Wherever you are this morning, the same thing is true. Christ Jesus made the most supreme sacrifice for YOU. Will you trust His definition of you or will you continue to rely on your own? The choice is yours.

## To the Broken

Standing on a busy street corner
all his possessions in his hand.
So many hurry all around him;
he feels like a stranger in this land.

In a cold, dark alley
she wakes for another day.
The loneliness that pierces her
seems to never go away.

It wasn't long ago
that he lived with his family.
Rejected for his incorrigibility
he now lives under a barren tree.

The drugs are slowly killing her.
She runs both to and from them.
Now she has abandoned all hope;
her prospects increasingly dim.

He turns his eyes upward
and sees the clouds overhead.
Darkness is a shroud for him;
he wishes that he was dead.

Stomach growls awaken her.
She hasn't eaten a proper meal in days.
She desires a way out of this hell
but she can't see through the maze.

He huddles in a dirty corner
fearing that he will soon die.
If only God would give him wings…
he dreams of the places he would fly.

She holds out her cup for some pity
and wears a sign around her neck.
"Please Help!" it says in black marker.
Inside and out she's a complete wreck.

Again he cries out to God
while inside he just holds on.
He fights with all that is within him
as he hopes for the new day to dawn.

Shattered and broken people
In the dark they are naked and cold.
Could it be Jesus who comforts them?
Could he be the one they hold?

Neglected by society around them;
they are the ones who remain unseen.
Lepers walking the lands of today,
They are forced to shout "unclean!"

Who will offer a kind word to them?
Who will comfort their souls?
Who will mend the broken places?
Who will patch all the holes?


When we look at people in these types of circumstances
it's easy to see that they are broken. Yet, there are so many more
who are broken and hiding. There are no overt indicators to our
brokenness. We put on our best masks to hide deep emotional pain.
We think it is far better to remain hidden and accepted for our
facade than it is to come out in the open and risk rejection.
I can identify with this logic. It was the way that I lived for years.
I put on the false smile and learned to live amongst the crowds. It
seemed like my best choice was just fitting in. Meanwhile, on the
inside I longed for something real. I longed for real relationships

with people, but most of all I longed for a relationship with God. I was certain that I wasn't worthy to have these things but after being broken by my shame yet again I called out his name. I found that, worthy or not, God did want to have a real and personal relationship with me. So friend, are you like me? What are the deepest desires of your heart? Sometimes it is when we are most broken that we become receptive to the idea of being made whole. Does this describe you?

## To the Weary and Broken

Like a beacon on the hill
there is a light pointing the way.
It appears brighter in the dark
than it does during the day.

To those trapped in blackness;
who travel with no direction
He knows your deep loneliness
and longs to give you affection.

He will not leave you alone
if you choose to call on His name.
His love will change you forever
and you will never be the same!

So come, you who are weary;
you who have lost your zest.
Lay your burdens down at His feet;
to find that in Him there is rest.

He will stand beside you
for the rest of your days.
He longs to lead and guide you
in all of His ways.

He will not leave or forsake you
even when you feel like you are lost.
He desires to have a relationship with you;
enough to pay a great cost.

So are you weathered and broken?
Trade it for the beauty in His name.
All your debts can be forgiven
so that you may live without blame.

Just as when we are in darkness we long for light, I believe the beauty of our brokenness is found in our longing to be made whole. Yet we cannot heal ourselves. We simply can't put together the broken pieces in our lives. To those of you who are broken this morning, if you never hear another word I say, hear this. There is one who knows your pain. He longs to step in and show you a better way. It requires that you reach out. It requires reaching for His hand. When you do that, you will find He is already reaching back! His name is Jesus and he is willing to meet you right in these places of brokenness, not to judge or condemn you, but to place his arms around you. He longs to embrace you and let you know that it will be ok. Will you place your trust in him?

## What Lies Ahead

Before me it sprawls,
so grand it escapes the eye,
Never beheld anything so tall.
from the ground clear into the sky.

Straining my eyes
catching a glimpse of the peak.
Firmly rooted down here
but it is the top that I seek.

Such beauty to behold,
such danger intertwined.
Mere mortal am I
Yet seeking the divine.

Must prepare for the climb
Must understand the way.
Yet aware of the dangers,
daunted by the investment of days.

I grab hold with confidence,
Solid ground under foot.
Grasping a tree for balance
It tears from the ground by the root!

Lying broken and defeated
I see before me a hand.
He reaches forward to steady me
And again I am able to stand.

He smoothes the way
Adds confidence to my stride
His convergence and unity
replace my doubt and divide.

Reaching the top
Barely able to catch my breath.
I am here standing
when I had faced certain death!

Oh my rock!
My shield and place of rest.
With confidence I can say,
That HE will always pass the test!

## When My Heart Grows Cold

When my heart grows cold
And the future looks bleak
When a lasting peace
Is all that I seek.

When I am confused
And shaken to the core.
When my need for mercy
Is met by a slamming door.

When I have no place to turn
And nowhere to confide
When fear grips me deeply
And I have nowhere to hide

When all that is within me
Is tattered and torn
When even my home
Is a place that is foreign

When my dreams are barren
In a land laid to waste
When my hope is gone
and my mind is erased.

When I cry out for the rocks
To cover up my shame.
When I want to run away
And even deny my name.

## Who I Once Was

When I was a child
you placed me on you knee
You patiently pointed out
the world for me to see.

When I was a youth
I tried to ignore your voice
I already knew the truth
but wanted to make my choice

When I was a teen
I began to run from you.
I wanted to ignore your existence
but I didn't have a clue.

When I was a man
I began to experience doubt
I found myself wondering
what this life was all about.

The shame of all these years
left me feeling isolated and alone
The pain of my choices
were cutting to the bone.

I ran and I hid,
still trying to avoid the pain.
The more that I ignored it
the more it remained the same.

Like a virus
I infected those around me.
Better to wear a mask
than to allow the world to see.

I was broken and flawed
I was afraid to trust.
Yet I never forgot your righteousness
and knew that you were just.

Why did you not leave me?
Why did you not turn your back?
Either way I am grateful
that you didn't let me fade to black.

I knew what I deserved;
an eternity of being lost.
But I forgot your perfect gift;
ignored how significant the cost.

Oh what a day
when I fell down on my face
When you reached out your hand
and extended your perfect grace!

I didn't deserve your forgiveness
I don't deserve unconditional love.
I don't deserve grace like rain
that falls from heaven above.

Still I won't question your forgiveness
I won't question your perfect will.
You took an empty vessel.
with your spirit you did fill.

The soul you created
went from broken to whole
The life I had destroyed
went from empty to full!

Sometimes the poetry I write is redundant. There is a reason for this. I carry only one true message. It is the message of our Savior. It is the message of the personal relationship that I have with him and the one he wants with you. It is the message of his love even in the face of our fallen nature. I sometimes question why it is that he would love me. I am TOTALLY undeserving! I laid to waste my own life for years. I infected those who got too close to me. My disease was contagious. How apt then is it that my healing is contagious as well? We all make a choice. I am grateful that God didn't leave me in the many wrong ones I made. He led me to a final choice that will remain with me for all of my days. He led me to his never ending love and grace!

## With The Rising Of The Sun

The moon has waned
while the sun has risen in the east.
You have taken time out for me
despite me being one of the least.

I look out before me
into a sea of grass waving in the wind.
Like the white caps upon the ocean
I watch as they rise and bend.

I am simply amazed
that You would meet me in this place.
I am surrounded by the beauty of Your creation
But none of these things compare to your Face.

For when You look down in love
I feel Your Spirit rising within me.
I don't hide it under a bushel
I set it high where the whole world can see.

I am not even important in these things
You can do it all without my assistance.
Yet You called me to bridge the divide
So those You love will not keep You at a distance.

The depths of your love are unfathomable.
The breadth of your grace is beyond comprehension.
You pursue the hearts of Your people
until You receive their full attention.

This servant would not know love
without first knowing Your love, my Master.
You found me slipping away in the storm
and rescued me from utter disaster.

No wave of the enemy will roll this boat.
No weapon formed by man shall prevail!
Your love is bigger than all the storms.
It is the only constant that does not fail!


For most of my life I believed I was "less than." I couldn't get living or religion right because of the fundamental flaws within me. Like everyone else, I wanted love. Yet in my eyes, love wasn't given freely, it was earned. I needed to do better and be better if He was going to love me. I needed to sin less and pray more. I needed a daily bible routine. I needed to find a way to stop the thoughts I was ashamed of. All of this pursuit through behavior modification failed. I couldn't do what it was that I wanted to do. I kept doing the things that I didn't want to do. In the end, like a dirty load of laundry, I found myself crumpled up on the floor.

It wasn't until the very foundation of my belief system crumbled beneath me that I learned the truth. I am not capable. I am not worthy and I am NOT good enough. He doesn't care. He knew I was never going succeed at my personal endeavors to become worthy. Little did I know that He loved me all along! The same is true of you, my friend. He has loved you all along. He's not waiting for you to fix yourself. He's waiting for you to trust Him. From this place of trust He can share with you His love… and you too will become a BELIEVER!

Have you found yourself holding onto a belief system like what I had? Are you tired of trying to earn His love? Slow down, take a deep breath and focus on His face. You will find that He is not only near, He's right there beside you!

## *YOU and me*

Let my name be hidden
so that your name may be blessed.
Let my days be restless
so that others may find rest.

Let my heart be still
so that yours may come in motion.
I am but a tidal pool
but you are my very ocean.

Let my face be shrouded
so that yours is in full view.
My message is old and stale.
Your message will renew.

Let my tongue be silent
so that yours can be fully heard.
I am but a mute.
Your message is the true word.

Let my eyes be blinded
so that they can fully see.
I may stumble in the darkness
but your light sets men free.

Let my ears be deaf
so that even when I cannot hear.
Your voice calls men away from pain.
Your voice frees men from fear.

Let my touch go unfelt
so that yours can't be ignored.
I may not feel pleasures
but you are meant to be adored.

Let my face fall to the floor
so that you may be raised on high.
I am the lowest of the low
but you make men's spirits fly.

Let me fall dead
So that others may be saved.
For I am dead without you
but you have risen from the grave.


I am weak and fall down. I fail and fall short. I break and
lack the ability to restore. I get tired and don't feel like going on.
I get depressed and feel like hiding. I am just like every man. You
can't rely on me. You can't put your hopes into my words. My
words were meant to do just one thing. They were meant to draw
you closer to the one who heals. They were meant to renew you
through the one who restores. I am merely a servant and a servant
is nothing without his master. My best advice is to bypass me and
go directly to the source of freedom, life and salvation. Do you
trudge through your days looking for hope? Do you look to tomor-
row to provide something that evaded you today? Worse yet, do
you fear tomorrow? A wise man once told me when you are uncer-
tain about what lies ahead, look up.

## You Hold the Keys

The sun is setting now
as my days come to their end.
Lord please forgive me of my transgressions
for I have sinned.

As I stepped out onto the water
I looked down at the waves.
I forgot the faith that you gave me
and the depth of your power to save.

Turning back to the boat for safety
I realized that it was too late.
If you don't grab my hand now
I will be left to this fate.

My heart desires more
than the certainty of solid ground.
Only you can perform miracles
Only in you can the impossible be found.

You lift me high
with a grace that I cannot afford.
Now I pray you lift me above this storm
As I call your name, my Lord.

For all who are held captive
only you hold the keys.
For all of us who are slaves to sin
it is your mercy that sets us free.

So swing open the prison gates
and call us out by name.
For once we are touched by true love
we can never be the same.

I was a true prisoner of my sin. I was locked away in a very dark place that was nearly devoid of light and expecting nothing more than what I deserved; a life sentence. But before the sun set and I was plunged into darkness for a final time I heard the jingle of keys. I dared not hope for what my heart truly wanted. Still, deep inside, I craved freedom. I longed for unconditional love but I did not feel worthy. None of my self prescribed solutions worked. I had relied on willpower before but it failed me. I made promises but I had broken them. I failed at all the self help religious rituals that I had been taught. I lacked faith. Yet I also lacked the blissful ignorance that once kept me blind. My only hope was his grace and his perfect love. As the sound of the keys grew closer my heart began to race. Surely he was coming to a cell next to mine. Surely the keys to freedom belonged to someone else. However, all doubt was dispelled when he called MY name!

Where are you today? Are you locked away in some dark cell? Do you long for freedom? What would you give to have your heart's true desire? Would you give it all? Would you give all of yourself? Once we are touched by true love we can never be the same. Will you allow him to touch your heart today? His name is Jesus and only he holds the keys!